LAST RANCHER STANDING

The Cliven Bundy Saga
A Close-up View

This standoff was not about cows, grazing fees, or taxes. It was about State sovereignty, disregard of Constitutional principles, tyrannical government, and—

"We the People"

Second Printing: February 2016

ISBN: 978-1-937735-84-5

Legends Library Publishing, Inc.
Rochester, NY

Inquiries to: info@legendslibrary.com
Phone: 877-222-1960
Website: www.LegendsLibrary.org

Cover design by Alisha Bishop

Note regarding photo credits: *We appreciate the many who took photographs and uploaded them to the Internet to inform the nation about what happened. Every effort was made to contact the copyright holder of each photograph used; however, in some cases we were not able to reach in person and so we have provided credits in every instance. We wish to thank those patriots who captured truth and evidence with one of the great modern-day weapons of peace, the camera.*

LAST RANCHER STANDING

The Cliven Bundy Saga
A Close-up View

Shawna Cox

New York

Dedication

This book is dedicated to the memory of Robert LaVoy Finicum, who was killed in the "line of duty" as a freedom fighter on January 26th 2016 outside of Burns, Oregon.

Contents

INTRODUCTION

Have you ever considered the reason our country is in such a state as we have now?

Quoting from Saul David Alinsky's book *Rules for Radicals: A Pragmatic Primer for Realistic Radicals*—

"There are 8 levels of control that must be obtained before you are able to create a socialist/communist state. The first is the most important."

1. Healthcare "Control healthcare and you control the people."
2. Poverty "Increase the Poverty level as high as possible." (Poor people are easier to control and will not fight back if you are providing everything for them to live.)
3. Debt "Increase the National Debt to an unsustainable level." (That way you are able to increase taxes, and this will produce more poverty.)
4. Gun Control "Remove the ability to defend themselves from the Government." (That way you are able to create a police state – total local control.)
5. Welfare "Take control of every aspect of their lives." (Food, livestock, housing, and income.)
6. Education "Take control of what people read and listen to and take control of what children learn in school."

7. <u>Religion</u> "Remove faith in God from the Government and school."

8. <u>Class Warfare</u> "Divide the people into the wealthy against the poor. Racially divide. This will cause more discontent and it will be easier to tax the wealthy with full support of the voting poor."

Background

Wild Mary

It was Sunday March 30, 2014 and I had decided it would be important for me to drive to Bunkerville, Nevada to see my friend Cliven Bundy. I had spoken to him a number of times since 1993 when he had taken the stand to refuse to sign a contract with the BLM (Bureau of Land Management) to manage him out of the ranching business. He was taking a stand because he knows that the Constitution Article 1 Section 8 states that Congress shall have the power—

To exercise exclusive Legislation in all Cases whatsoever, over such District (not exceeding ten Miles square) as may, by Cession of particular States, and the Acceptance of Congress, become the Seat of the Government of the United States, and to exercise like Authority over all Places purchased by the Consent of the Legislature of the State in which the Same shall be, for the Erection of Forts, Magazines, Arsenals, dock-Yards, and other needful Buildings;

Where does the Federal Government have a right to control State Lands and especially police those lands?

<u>Provisions of the Constitution</u>

The major provisions of the Constitution are as follows:

***First:* Sovereignty lies in the people themselves. Every governmental system has a sovereign, one or several who possess all the executive, legislative, and judicial powers. That sovereign may be an individual (king), a group (state), or the people themselves.**

The Founding Fathers believed in common law, which holds that true sovereignty rests with the people. Believing this to be in accord with truth, they inserted this imperative in the Declaration of Independence: "To secure these rights life, liberty, and the pursuit of happiness, governments are instituted among men, deriving their just powers from the consent of the governed."

The First Emergency

In 1995 with five children in high school, I was one of the few PTA Board Members on hand the morning it all began. It was 8:15 a.m. and we had already started our meeting when Karla, the County Clerk, rushed into the room out of breath and in a panic. She half hollered at us as she explained that she needed our help, right now! There were no elected officials in our town at the time and she had just received a phone call that indicated that President Clinton had just issued a statement regarding a new National Monument comprising over two million acres that would encompass the whole city of Kanab, Utah and half of Kane County! None of our State Representatives, elected officials or even the governors of Utah nor Arizona knew anything about it! We made a quick plan.

We split up and began to contact all the business owners in town to come to an emergency meeting in the basement of the Red Hills Motel downtown. We literally shut the town down! During that meeting I learned about an environmental group that I had never heard of before called the "Grand Canyon Trust Company." We made plans to contact the media, our state and local officials and every person in the town to rally together to see what we could do to STOP this. It would be devastating to our town that has been here for over 100 years. How could one man take away our livelihood, our hard work, and our heritage with just a stroke of the pen? Who in this world could do that? What country did we live in anyway? So many of our local friends and families has fought in World War 1, WW2, Korean War and so many others to protect our freedoms and our rights, how could this happen? We were in shock. My mind went back again to Article 1, sec.8.

Membership Roster

I hurried to my business office and jumped on the internet to research the Grand Canyon Trust Company, based in Moab, Utah. I not only found it but discovered it was an environmental group headed up by a man named Bill Hedden. When I pulled up their membership roster I was shocked to see that a huge percent of the members were from China! What? The pieces to the puzzle began to take shape in my mind. We had spent over 20 years trying to open the Kaparowitz coal mine, working through all the red government tape and now that we were getting ready to sink the first shaft the following week—since being shut down in 1974—they pulled this? Does that mean that Clinton has sold us to China so he could be re-elected as the US President for a second term, or was there more to it? I printed out the membership roster and rushed back to the motel to see if anyone was still there. Roger was on his way back to Salt Lake City. I showed him the paper and he too was in shock! He took the list to Salt Lake with him and the very next day on the major news we heard how President Bill Clinton had sold us out to China. That was only published far and wide for approximately two days before someone had it removed from the media!

<u>Second</u>: To safeguard these rights, the Founding Fathers provided for the separation of powers among the three branches of government – the legislative, the executive, and the judicial.

The use of checks and balances was deliberately designed, first, to make it difficult for a minority of the people to control the government, and second, to place restraint on the government itself.

Local Sheriffs

The first time I met Cliven and his son Ryan Bundy they had come over to Kanab to speak to our group. We had organized and formed "People for the USA" to stand up against this tyranny. Cliven was one of our guest speakers about the Constitution and explained how important it was for our County Sheriff to back us up and support us because he has more power than the President of the United States and we don't have to allow this to happen. I was really impressed with him and his convictions. I wanted to learn more.

In order for people to prosper, they cannot afford to spend their time constantly guarding family, fields, and property against attack and theft, so they join together with their neighbors and hire a sheriff. At this precise moment, government is born. The individual citizens delegate to the sheriff their unquestionable right to protect themselves. The sheriff now does for them only what they had a right to do for themselves, nothing more.

Quoting from Bastiat: *"If every person has the right to defend – even by force – his person, his liberty, and his property, then it follows that a group of men have the right to organize and support a common force to protect these rights constantly. This the principle of collective right – its reason for existing, its lawfulness – is based on individual right."*

Unilateral Confiscation

Chris Cannon was our State Representative at the time. He knew nothing about the creation of the Monument until the day we had received the phone call. He was actually on the phone with Bill Clinton the night and early morning hours as Bill told Chris that he wasn't sure what he was going to do yet, but in fact boarded the plane about 6 am to fly to the South Rim of the Grand Canyon to make the official declaration that same morning.

My mother was the Mayor of Fredonia and my friend Karen Alvey was the Mayor of Kanab at the time. They both had official invitations to attend along with a number of others from our community leaders.

We had black ribbons pinned to all of our shirts as a symbol of mourning. We put together a wonderful assembly at the local high school auditorium to begin at the exact time that Clinton was on the South Rim dedicating *our* land. He didn't even have enough courage to come to Kanab. We were told that he was afraid he would be assassinated. That was uncalled for—nobody had even thought such a thing. We had all the major media here and they aired our assembly which were patriotic and historical stories, a few elected official speeches and some of the best patriotic songs and music you would ever hear. There were tears of sadness and unbelief. We let go masses of black balloons out on the football field. We had received numerous calls from liberals who told us that we were "brainwashing" our children if we let them out of school to attend this display and such nonsense. During the meeting it was opened up to questions and I stood up and asked, "So if they are taking one million acres, just where are the boundaries?" We still had yet to see the plans on paper. The TV media actually did record what I said, they aired my standing to ask a question and then in bold banner across the screen printed: "CLINTON BASHERS." That's how the media twists things in the minds of the public.

We citizens of Kanab and Kane County have been through some tremendous fights from the beginning of the creation of the Grand Staircase Escalante Monument. It took months to figure out where the boundaries were. It ended up after zigzagging around a few properties who opposed the takeover, the total amount of land stolen was 1.8 million acres. Our sheriff and county commissioner went out and tore down all the road signs the BLM had put up on our county roads that stated this was GSENM and had numbered our roads. They were threatened with charges, arrest, and fines. The Federal Government came in and took over our lands without any permission from the state whatsoever. They tried to close down all of our county roads and steal our own private properties. When we screamed and yelled they offered to pay us Fair Market Value for our homes and private properties. My question was, "How much? The Fair Market Value before you made the Monument or after? What if we don't want to sell, then you can just steal it?"

Kate Cannon Conspiracy

After going through years of hell trying to save Kanab, Kane County and our RS2477 roads that had been granted to us by Congress, we have finally begun to win back some of our roads just this last year. We must give thanks to the valiant effort of our County Commissioners led by Mark Habbeshaw with the help of our Local Sheriff Lamont Smith and our State Representative, Mike Noel.

One morning while I was working the front desk of our motel my dear friend Mary Bulloch Rucker, a very tough cowgirl who had just been widowed, came rushing in. She begged me to come with her because she needed a witness of the abuse she was receiving from the head of the BLM, Kate Cannon. Mary was clutching her chest as she explained that she had just been to the hospital to see the doctor because of all the chest pains she was having. She told me it was the stress that Kate had been putting her under. Apparently Kate was declaring there was a drought on the 50 mile mountain where Mary and her late husband Boyd had their Cattle Grazing Allotment. Kate wanted Mary to remove all of her cattle from off the land. Mary's herd are wild cows who eat browse and grasses. They are used to this terrain and thrive thereon. It is true there had been no rain for weeks but there was one waterhole down at the bottom of the mountain by her holding corals that did have water in it. Kate told the BLM employees to go out and fence off the waterhole which action caused Mary's cattle in the lower section to thirst to death. Kate had sent helicopters to watch the water hole and as soon as one of Mary's cattle crossed the fence to drink, Kate would hit Mary with a trespass fee of $650. It was insane!

Mary had driven her cattle truck in from the ranch a couple of times to pay the trespass fees. The county road was so rough because the county was waiting for rain before it would send a grader out there to blade it. Mary could only drive 5 miles an hour it was so wash boarded. She ended up breaking her truck axle two different times because of it and had to walk for help many miles because there are very few if any people who travel that desolate land.

Mary had been to the BLM office just before she went to the hospital in hopes of trying to reason with Kate. Kate's response was, "If you can't handle it then sell out!" After Mary came out of the hospital there was a note tucked inside her driver's window that said, "Grand Canyon Trust Company will buy your ranch, talk to Bill Heddon," and had his phone number on it.

That is why she came to me begging for help! She wanted me to go with her to visit Kate and be a witness to their conversation. I did not know Kate personally and I was dressed in a pair of bib-overalls. I had a little voice recorder and slipped it into my front pocket as we headed to the BLM office.

When we arrived I went into Kate's room with Mary. I didn't say anything because Mary again asked Kate why she would give her the number to Bill Hedden, did they have some hidden agenda that they were working together. Mary said her ranch was

NOT FOR SALE! Then she tried again to explain to Kate that in a couple of months when the water began to flow down the dry river beds from up on the top of the mountain then she would be able to drive her cattle down but not until they had water because they would all die of thirst in the dry desert. Mary told her again that the cattle had plenty of feed and water up on top but Kate refused to listen. She demanded that Mary bring them down now! Mary told Kate that if she wanted her to get the cattle down then Kate could bring water troughs full of water and disperse them every few miles so the cattle wouldn't die. Kate said Mary should bring the cattle and she would get the water. Mary said, "You get the water and I will bring the cattle." They went back and forth about bringing the water first or the cattle. It was like a cat fight power struggle. Nothing was resolved that day.

Due to the trespass fees, Mary had been sleeping by the gate near the waterhole to keep the cattle out. There was just no way. The cattle were so thirsty that they were dropping their newborn calves and leaving them to die to search for water. It was horrible!

I tried to ask for the help from the leadership in a People for the USA meeting, but until I started yelling trying to get some of the men to understand the magnitude of the problem Mary was facing they were not listening. I hate to say this but men have an ego problem I have had to deal with for years. They just don't listen to women until you can get their attention first, kind of like a donkey. I explained to the other ranchers that because Mary was the weak link and the first ranch coming into Kane County they would take her down first and then they would go after the next ranch and pick them off one at a time. They would ALL fall like dominoes. The intent was to get rid of all the ranches by turning them into willing sellers using fees and restrictions so the BLM could get the cattle off the land. It has been a plan of the environmental groups for years. At last they got the picture and agreed to help Mary. A few of the local cowboys went in to explain to Kate about leaving them on top until the first of October but she would hear none of it!

I was at the motel one evening when I received a call from a rancher in Escalante. He stated that Kate had hired some local cowboys to go drive Mary's cattle off the mountain. None of them would do it because they said Mary would kill them and they were afraid of her. She had a couple of nick names: "Bloody Mary" and "Wild Cow Mary". She was one tough talker. Kate told them that Mary was in jail and wouldn't be up on the Mountain. I think the phone call was to see if that was the truth. When I heard that I couldn't help but chuckle. I turned to Mary and said, "Did you know that you were in jail?" as I handed her the phone. Needless to say the cowboys refused to help Kate Cannon rustle Mary's cattle.

Evidence Gathering

I helped Mary out with a place to stay and legal aid. Together we loaded up her truck and horses and headed to the Fifty Mile Mountain to take pictures we needed for evidence. We drove five miles or less per hour as we traveled that rough dusty road. About midnight we stopped and threw our sleeping bags out on the dusty ground and went to sleep.

The next morning we arrived at the corals and unloaded the horses, unloaded all the supplies, and weighed everything we loaded into blankets for packing on the horses. We each had a horse to ride with bedrolls and saddle bags then we each had another horse to lead packed with feed and supplies. The packs had to be weighed exactly for balance as the trail was very steep and treacherous. It took a long time to get loaded but with long sleeve shirts and cowboy hats with hurricane straps we headed out. I had my video camera rolling as we climbed the "Devil's Backbone". It is a blue clay mountain that is very steep on either side, hundreds of feet down to the bottom. If you slide off you and your horse will surely meet your deaths. The trail on top was very narrow and we had one younger horse that had not ridden this more than once so Mary gave the new horses shots to keep them calm. I took lots of video.

As we got off the Backbone we had other challenges and I followed along behind Mary on the narrow trail across the face of another steep mountain. At one point there was a place in the trail that had eroded with the rain and she told me to jump it. I wasn't sure about the pack horse behind me but I did as I was told. I made it, but the pack horse lost his balance and began to slide and my horse started bucking! Mary yelled at me jump off and run on the path pulling my horse to give footing to the pack horse. It was Mary's territory and I did as I was told. We made it! Normally I would have ridden a bucking horse until I gained control but I knew Mary was experienced at this so I listened and obeyed!

Next we traveled through the briars so thick I had to duck my head to protect my eyes as the brush would grab at my face. I was very grateful for long sleeves. At one point the brush ripped my hat off anyway and as I grabbed hold of it I noticed that the cotton batting from the pack blankets was being torn off our packs along the way.

At each different turn there seemed to be a new adventure. At the slick steep red rocks ledge that dropped off many feet below, Mary told me of a time when a rider and his horse had been gored by a wild cow that had come back up the rope and of a cowboy that fell to his death from the very ledge we were riding on. It was pitch black by the time we reached the top of the canyon. I couldn't see my hand in front of my face. I could hear Mary up ahead and just hoped she knew where she was going. At last we came to a fence and somehow she found the gate and let us in.

We ended up at a little rustic old cabin. We unsaddled the horses and just let them go free. We got inside the cabin and tried to find a candle to light. The rats had chewed up everything including ice chests, candles, everything. She did bring a new candle with which we were able to see while we threw out our sleeping bags on the cots that were there. She then informed me that the mice would be running through all night and I should cover my face with my hat. I hated mice and thought this has to be the worst! I asked her why she wasn't covering her face with her hat and she told me that her dog we had with us was really good at catching and killing the mice. As I pulled my sleeping bag clear up around my face the best I could and parked my hat on top I wondered how I was going to be able to sleep. I thought I was going to suffocate.

Sure enough, as daylight began to break through the walls the next morning, where there used to be chinking there began to be a parade of mice as they literally filed in and across the logs on practically each row. That was it; I climbed out of my bag and ran outside. All the mice must have been inside because I didn't see any outside. The horses were there and they came in for feed. I put some grain in their feed bag but one of them took off with the feed bag still on his head. I called to him but he wouldn't come to me. I went to wake up Mary. When I told her he ran off with the feed bag she jumped up and told me that if he went for water with the bag on his face he could drown himself. Now I felt terrible and we went out to find him. Luckily he came to her as she coaxed him along and she was able to remove the bag.

Mary had brought her six shooters along, half expecting some cowboys or federal agents to show up and take shots at us. We proceeded with caution having no idea who we might encounter. I took video of the beautiful grass and streams full of running water. You would not know there was a drought from up here. The cattle were happy and fat. We rode around the ranch and fixed fences here and there. It was a beautiful day.

I had to leave before dark to catch a flight in Salt Lake so Mary and I rode down the rocky back side toward Escalante to meet my husband in his truck. As we were pulling away I felt sad to leave watching Mary lead my horse behind her back up the rugged mountain. My husband and I noticed helicopters arriving at the reservoir, dipping buckets to haul water for the cattle drive the next day. The local cowboys were supposed to come and help drive the cattle in the morning. I left with a heavy heart, but I already had made my travel arrangements months earlier and couldn't change them.

The cowboys did show up and it was a terrible hot and dusty drive. The poor cattle were so stressed out that they were going crazy because they were being driven hard and didn't have time to drink as much as they needed because the cowboys wanted to get them down as quickly as possible. They knew it was only a matter of time that they were going to lose the cows if they didn't hurry.

There were BLM helicopters overhead and as they reached the gate late in the day there were numbers of environmentalists perched upon the fences pounding their fists on the fence rails chanting "Cattle Free, 2003. Cattle Free, 2003." The cowboys were angry and upset.

The cows were loaded into cattle trucks and were so stressed out they were stomping each other to death. One of my very good friends and a mild-mannered man, David, for probably the first time in his life, swore at the people chanting on the fences and crawled underneath the shade of his truck bed and wept!

The BLM-hired cowboys unloaded the cattle in the lower corrals where they had brought some hay. These cattle had never eaten hay in their lives.

Later we learned that Kate Cannon was trying to get the Branding Inspector, Raymond Christensen, to inspect the cattle over to her so she could transport them. It was illegal for him to inspect someone else's cattle over to anyone other than the owner. He refused to do it!

I had returned home by now and during the night we got word that Kate had hired some other cowboys to load the cattle up into cattle trucks for hauling them to the Salina, Utah Livestock Auction for sale the next morning. They couldn't go through the Port-of-Entry with uninspected cattle so they were driving them up the back dirt roads. We alerted our Sheriff and Attorney plus all our cowboys and headed out. I had to stay and man the phones. (We didn't have cell phones then.) We contacted the Auction and threatened to put him out of business if he sold any of the rustled cattle. We also called every cattleman and buyer we knew and informed them that the BLM was trying to sell stolen cattle. When everyone arrived at the auction, the BLM and their attorneys were there along with our Sheriff and attorneys and cowboys and cattle trucks and Mary! It was a show down. It really came to a standstill because who was breaking the law?

<u>Third</u>: The powers the people granted to the three branches of government were specifically limited.

Permitting few powers to the Federal Government, these chiefly being the powers concerning "war, peace, negotiation and distributing to everyone exactly the functions he is competent to. Let the national government be entrusted with the defense of the nation, and its foreign and federal relations; the State governments with the *civil rights*, law, police, and administration of what concerns the State generally, the counties with the local concerns of the counties, and each ward direct the interests within itself.

It is by dividing and subdividing these republics from the great national one down through all its subordination... that all will be done for the best.

What has destroyed liberty and the rights of man in every government which has ever existed? It is generalizing and concentrating all functions and powers into one body. The Founding Fathers well understood human nature and its tendency to exercise unrighteous dominion when given authority. A Constitution was therefore designed to limit government to certain enumerated functions, beyond which was tyranny.

Stand-off

The question at hand was, "Who has the proper authority? Federal BLM or the County government?

From Mary's own account she told me that while they all stood around trying to figure out who was in charge, she went into the corrals and called to Oscar, her giant gray Brahma bull. Everyone was afraid of Oscar because he looked so mean! But Mary and he were buddies. Mary whistled for Oscar, calling him by name, and single-handedly led Oscar with the cows right behind him into the waiting cattle trucks. She then gathered up the cowboys and they jumped into their trucks and hauled off the cattle and hid them so the BLM couldn't take them again.

This really put Mary out of business as now she owed for hay to feed the cows, supplies for the round up, and suffered personal health problems because of the stress. She really had no way to pay for all this because her income had just been destroyed. After going to court and having us testify that the feral cattle were hers from off her ranch, the government finally paid her for them. Kate Cannon was transferred to another location.

Government employees immune from prosecution

If you will research you will discover that even if you try to sue anyone who works for the government (such as a police officer who has stepped across the line), they will be put on administrative leave with or without pay. The worst thing that happens to them is they lose their job. You might get a settlement if you sue your city but then you are raising your taxes on yourself and friends. What about someone who works for the city or county that you didn't elect. The only way to get rid of them is to threaten the elected official who hired them. Even on State phone answering machines you will find that they say: "You cannot hold us accountable for wrongful information you receive from our employees." Just call the Motor Vehicle Division in Phoenix, Arizona for example. It's OK for the police to lie to you and entrap you but if you lie you can be charged with a crime. In fact they try to make you lie to prove you are guilty of something you are not; they call it plea bargaining. They'll give you a lesser charge after they charge you with multiple offenses first making you believe that is your best option, the lesser of two evils.

Mary was with us for two more years and became a celebrity at the Kane County Western Legends where she met a wonderful "National Hall of Fame" musician, Curley Muskgrave who wrote a song about her and the Fifty Mile Mountain.

The public doesn't understand the reason all the wilderness study areas were created in the first place. It has been to get the people off the land. The Federal Government cannot control people who have the freedom to sustain themselves on the land. If they create a Monument then gradually create buffer zones bigger and wider to encompass more land, add permit requirements with hefty fines and imprisonment threats to control access until you finally restrict access altogether. It pushes the free people into the cities where they can have better control of them. They have restricted our access here on our Monument area to "4 heart beats." That means no more family outings, hikes, horse rides etc. and no large groups such as Boy Scouts, Film Making, Church groups because 4 heartbeats also counts as 1 for the horse, one for the dog, and two people or two people and two horses for examples.

The new head of the BLM came and I connected him with Mary, who had returned home to be with her family in Cedar City. I don't how much money they finally ended up settling with her, but she only lived a couple more years and passed away from the health problems she received because of government overstepping its authority. (Another victim of tyrannical government!)

***Fourth*: Our Constitutional government is based on the principle of representation.**

The principle of representation means that we have delegated to an elected official the power to represent us. The Constitution provides for both direct and indirect representation. Both forms of representation provide a tempering influence on pure democracy. The intent was to protect the individual's and the minority's rights to life, liberty, and the fruits of their labors – property. These rights were not to be subject to majority vote.

We need to repeal the 17th Amendment that allows the Senators of a State to be voted on instead of being appointed. We lost our check and balance of power in the House of Representatives.

We should have a Republican form of government, not a Democracy!

Supporters

I served as secretary of the *People for the USA* group we formed. We had a roads committee who valiantly GPSed all the roads. We elected one of our own, Mike Noel, a former BLM employee who became our State Representative. We hired a young Constitutional Attorney by the name of Mike Lee. He did such an excellent job in representing us that I personally did all I could to help get him elected as the Utah State Senator to represent us in Washington DC. He votes strictly constitutional.

We owe a great deal to these wonderful men and all their sacrifices for our city and county and the freedoms we are winning back. Most of all we owe our thanks and gratitude to our Father in Heaven. God has blessed us over and over with one miracle after another. Our whole community would pray for intervention by Him many times.

A Moral Duty

Now maybe you can understand why I had to help Cliven. Two years ago, April 4, 2012, I had received a message on my telephone answering service from him explaining that early on Wednesday morning the Federal Government was going to come to his ranch and start confiscating his cattle. He was pleading for help to come and bring all of our friends and cowboys because he had all of his children and grandchildren there and he would do "Whatever it Takes" to stop them!

Cliven and Carol Bundy

What does "Whatever it Takes" mean? I asked myself? I was in the middle of one of our Tea Party Committee meetings when I opened the email and read it. This was Tuesday night prior and it was already 7 p.m. I went into a panic! How do I help him? Who can I gather together that quickly before morning? Should we, or could we bring guns? What are the state laws about carrying guns in Nevada? As all these questions raced through my mind, there was not a minute to lose! I could picture a bloody massacre just like Waco, Texas. That was in Texas where the government had gone in and shot, killed, and then burned down a home filled with peaceful Branch Davidians who just wanted to worship their own way and had been villainized by the major media to cover up and give an excuse to why the government ordered the slaughter of innocent men, women and children.

Every State should have the right to open carry any gun or weapon according to the 2nd Amendment. It is legal to open carry in Nevada. Permit holders can carry concealed weapons.

The Alabama Constitution Article 1, sec. 35 describes it best: "The sole object and only legitimate end of government is to protect the citizen in the enjoyment of life, liberty, and property, and when the government assumes other functions it is usurpation and oppression."

I began to contact everyone I knew in the political world who might have some kind of influence to stop this usurpation and oppression. I contacted Utah officials clear to the Governor's office and then those in the Nevada Senate and everyone in between I could reach. I even drove down to Arizona and contacted some of the Bundy Family members pleading for help. I prayed that people who had influence could and would step up. One of my Senator friends told me to take a breath and calm down just a little and call so and so. I did and the ball started rolling. By early next morning I received a call that the Federal Agents had backed off but I was assured it wasn't forever, it was just being postponed for another day. I was so relieved. It would at least give us time to figure out some kind of defense.

The Saga Begins

And so it began again. On about Tuesday March 25, 2014, almost two years from his last call, I received a call from Cliven asking me to gather up groups of people in groups of twenty-five to come with their horses and trailers, prepared to stay for about a four-day shift, after which we could rotate another group in and out. He said he would be prepared to feed them and their horses if they had things to sleep in, such as tents and trailers. They needed help.

I began to assess just how many people I could get to go. They all had jobs and had to work to keep the wolf away from the door, so to speak. This economy has really been hard on the working class citizens living hand to mouth. My cowboys that rode with us to help with the Wild Cow Mary Saga were 20 years older and some of them were now passed on and some in wheel chairs, on oxygen and suffering other complications. I decided I needed to go to Cliven's ranch and assess the situation before hand so I would know exactly what the best plan of defense would be—one that might do the most good with the people whom I was able to recruit.

It was Sunday afternoon of March 30th and after we left our church services, I talked one of my dear friends into driving with me to Bunkerville. We took the exit to Bunkerville and after we crossed the bridge over the river we hung a right on the dusty gravel road as we followed the Melons for Sale signs. When we turned into the Bundy's Ranch we were met by all kinds of old farm equipment and things piled around so that you couldn't really see the house. As we followed the winding road we passed over a little bridge and came upon the Ranch house. It looked just like a ranch house you would have pictured in your mind. There was a wooden bench swing hanging in the front yard along with a horse swing for the kids made out of an old tire that was hanging from a tree limb. There were flower pots with flowers in bloom on the porch with an old cowboy dinner bell mounted by the door.

(credit huffingtonpost.com)

When the big wooden front door opened we were greeted with open arms and a hearty welcome. Among the friendly smiles and hugs we were offered a seat on the brown leather couch and chairs that surround the living room walls with the usual brick-faced fireplace in the middle. On the walls were pictures of their whole family of 13 children with their spouses and all the grandchildren. Another picture featured the St. George temple. All through the house were wonderful sayings that would touch your heart like "Cowboys don't take baths, they just dust off" mounted in the bathroom. Needless to say, they made you feel right at home. You could say, that everyone who enters there can "feel the Love."

Cliven and Carol on the brown leather couch *(credit youviewed.com)*

Bundy Family

Cliven and his wife, Carol, along with a couple of their children and grandchildren, were in the living room. I explained that we had come to get a visual of exactly how we could see what would be most effective strategically. When Cliven told me the cattle gathering was supposed to begin on the 6th of April, which was the next Sunday, it surprised me that the BLM would pick that particular day to begin, after all it was the Sabbath Day.

The Bundy Family

Contract to Steal

Carol showed me the contract between the BLM and a cowboy from Utah by the name of Shayne Sampson for the sum of $966,000 to gather 1,100 head of Cliven Bundy's cattle. Cliven told me that he didn't have that many cattle. He said that he only claimed 500 head and there were possibly another 100 head of new calves that had not been branded yet. He told me also that the BLM had planned to sell the cows at the "R" Livestock Auction in Richfield, Utah. I could hardly believe my ears. We had already been through that with Mary's cattle at the Salina auction over 20 years ago when the Head of the BLM, Kate Cannon, had rustled them. You would think that NO auction house would dare to touch "rustled" cattle. There are very strict laws about that still on the law books today, at least all over the West.

Liberty sign
(credit huffingtonpost.com)

Cliven and the kids showed me the big 50-foot poles that they had built with a huge sign that reads "Liberty—Freedom—For God We Stand" with "We The" and "People" metal tops ready to be erected. The plan was to install them up on the plateau by Interstate 15 so all the people could see them from the freeway. It would also be located not far from the compound the BLM had begun to set up. Cliven said that the day before, which was Saturday, as he was driving around the ranch with the news woman from Las Vegas channel 13, they accidentally came upon the compound already being installed. The corral panels were up and there had been a number of one-ton hay bales already delivered.

I asked Cliven how long he thought it would take them to gather a trailer full of cattle. He explained to me that it took him a few weeks to gather that many because of how far they had to travel to round them up. As a plan was forming in my mind, I left Cliven with the understanding that when the BLM had gathered a trailer full of cattle that he would keep an eye on them and let me know so that I could gather a huge group together to protest at the Utah Port of Entry and not allow the cattle to even come into our state. That would be easy for me to do.

As we drove home Cliven explained to me where the compound was being set up. So, on the return trip we took a couple of pictures as we blew by.

EPISODE ONE

❧

Assault and Arrest

At home I began to contact people and get them ready to head for St. George with just a last minute notice. We made signs and contacted people in Hurricane, St. George, Cedar City and elsewhere.

During the week I made a number of calls to Mike, my state representative, and he informed me that he had information that the cattle gathering had been changed to the 4th of April, which to me really made much more sense. I was also told the Utah State legislature and governor were trying to keep them out of Utah. Another bit of information was that the owner of the "R" Livestock Auction had been prepaid (I call it a bribe) to sell the cattle there. The amount was unknown but was first rumored about $100,000, then someone said it was more like $300,000, and the last figure I heard was more like $48,000 because he had to build some corrals to keep the cattle in. The owner, Scott Robins, a young family man, was behind on some property taxes and needed the money.

Disperse!

I called the Bundy's to check in a time or two but nothing more was happening than the BLM posting signs and driving the roads. It was General Conference weekend beginning Saturday April 5. Sunday the 6th the last session of conference was over and right after that at approximately 4:30 p.m. Dave Bundy, Cliven's third son was with his wife and five children along with his brother Ryan and his wife with five of their seven children and sister Bailey were driving out of the Ranch when they noticed a whole caravan of BLM vehicles coming down out of the Gold Butte Mountain. There were approximately eight to ten white SUVs followed by three one-ton trucks pulling cattle trailers behind them, followed by eight to ten more white SUVs. They pulled over on the side of the State Highway SR 71 and began to take photos with their cell phones, cameras and Dave had an iPad. They were all standing outside of their vehicles and as the first of the SUVs pulled onto the black top they stopped, jumped out with guns, teasers and attack dogs (German shepherds). They were yelling at the families to "Get back in your cars, and DISPERSE" with lights flashing and using their bull horn. They told some local vehicles to disperse and move on. What? They were not interfering whatsoever. What did that mean to DISPERSE? They had all been taught the Constitution and knew that they had a First Amendment right to stand on a public road (even a State Highway) and take pictures. They were doing nothing wrong!

The Bill of Rights, Article 1 - "Congress shall make no law respecting an establishment of religion or prohibiting the free exercise thereof, or abridging the freedom of speech, or of the press, or the right of the people peaceably to assemble and to petition the Government for a redress of grievances.

Dave explained to them that he knew his first amendment rights! Dave just kept taking pictures as the armed men with barking dogs on leashes, forced the woman and children back into their cars at gun point. Dave didn't argue but didn't move and continued to take video footage with his iPad. Then the armed men all turned, encircling Dave. Angie said that she got back in her car with her children because the armed men forced them to but she refused to drive off because Dave was still standing there and not getting into his car. She was not about to leave him there alone. Dave turned slowly and sat his iPad on the hood of his car as he realized the men intended to carry out their threat to arrest him. As he turned around the man on his right rushed in about the same time as the man to his left and they both grabbed hold of his arms one at a time and began to pull him to the left and to the right, like a tug of war.

Then a third one came in and began kicking and punching Dave in the stomach. He said he knew he was going down and didn't want to go down very fast and didn't want to put his face in the gravel so even though two men were holding his arms, he was strong enough to pull his flattened hands in front of his face to protect himself from eating the gravel. I believe it was because cowboys are raised to work hard, ride, rope and throw cattle that he had the strength to do this. Dave said after he was on the ground the men kept yelling for him to put his arms behind his back and with a dog barking in his ear he saw they were about to tase him so he gave up his left arm. The men grabbed it and twisted it up violently as another man put his knee into his neck and one on his head. They were trying to pull his other arm out from under his face and as they did, the man kneeling on his head began to grind Dave's face into the gravel with his knee and then with his foot. Dave said that at that point he was really hoping they would hurry and get him arrested because he was in a lot of pain. All the little children and relatives were watching this transpire and taking photos. The children and women were in shock and upset! As the men pulled Dave to his feet he remembers staring at the name tag of the man who ground his face into the gravel. Dave looked directly in his eyes and said, "I would like to meet you in an alley; nobody grinds my face into the gravel and gets away with it; I will find you." Dave remembers his name tag reading "J. Cox."

Dave was arrested and hauled off in the back of a truck to the compound yard at Toquop Wash. He was held there for approximately 3 1/2 hours where they paraded him around like a trophy on display, taking pictures, etc. A woman who acted like she was in charge by the name of Lisa Wilson got into the passenger seat of the truck and began asking questions. Dave said he didn't have to answer anything to her. "To me," she said, "I am Officer Wilson" to which Dave replied, "To me, you are nothing!" They headed to Henderson, Nevada to incarcerate him at the facility there. The whole time they had Dave he questioned and tried to teach his assailants about the Constitution and the Bill of Rights. He even asked the men who were transporting him to Henderson if they had taken an Oath of Office to defend and uphold the Constitution. One man finally answered and said he thinks so, but upon questioning they had no clue as to what that had taken an Oath to uphold. One man did say he thinks he might have read the Constitution once. He was totally ignored as the two men carried on their own conversation. Dave didn't give up but continued to try to educate the men about the Constitution all the way.

Once they found the jail, they drove around the block three or four times trying to find the entrance. It was at this time that Dave said to them, jokingly, "Well it looks like one of you might have to just chain me up in your garage over night!" The officers did chuckle at that for the first time. Then finally the one officer said, "Oh, we almost forgot to read you your Miranda rights" and proceeded to do so. After they finished Dave said, "It doesn't really matter because you don't have the authority to do that anyway." Dave said he was mad but he tried to calm down and get control of himself. After they booked him into jail, Dave even tried to educate the young 20 year-old heroin addict that was his cell mate.

It was dark and cold in that cell as he lay on the cold hard steel bunk with nothing but a jumpsuit and a small blanket. He began to have lots of feelings of uncertainty. "Am I a criminal?" he asked himself. He thought: Tonight I am in the custody of the City but what about tomorrow when I will be in Federal custody. With the new NDAA passed there is a chance they could keep me for a very long time. His thoughts were turned to his family, his wife and children. What will become of them? He got up a few times in the night and tried to open the door. He couldn't bear the thought of not being with his family.

He felt ashamed before the Lord as he knelt in prayer. Why is it that I don't pray as often as I should when things are going well and then I pour my heart out when everything is bearing down upon me? I knelt and prayed a lot, then I began to sing hymns. I didn't care who heard me. I needed the Lord and He brought me the peace I was looking for. I knew My Heavenly Father (my Lord) was there.

The Non-Hearing and Reunion

The next morning they came and put handcuffs on Dave, cinching them so tight his hands began to swell. Being a big guy, Dave was put in the back seat of the police SUV behind the metal mesh plate in a seat that was too short to put his knees in and causing terrible pain. He would try to lean forward on his forehead to relieve the awful pressure on his bound-up hands and arms. He asked them to please release his arms or to loosen them because it created terrible pain and was very inhumane but his pleas fell on deaf ears. They also had put him in an orange jumpsuit and had leg cuffs on his ankles so tight they made his feet swell. They led him up and down to different rooms to be questioned by different people.

After waiting about an hour to see the Federal judge, suddenly an officer came into the room, handed Dave two citations, removed the cuffs, shackles and chains and his orange jumpsuit, returned his personal belongings they had removed from his pockets, gave him a sack lunch, and released him through a door onto the streets of Las Vegas. He had no money, no cell phone, and no iPad, but was now free to leave. He felt like a vagrant but was happy to see the sunlight! The citations were for *failure to disperse and avoiding arrest*.

He wandered down the street looking for a pay phone. Not many of those any more. He finally did come across one but didn't have any money for the phone even if the person on the phone would ever get off. After a little while a woman who came in to get gas was willing to let Dave use her phone after he offered to buy some gas for her car. Thank goodness for credit cards!

He called his Dad and said he was never so happy to see that old truck coming down the road and there was his Dad! He was ever so grateful! The iPad and cell phone were never recovered.

The day was Monday April 7th the same day I returned with two of my other friends, Lon and Vikilee to check things out. I had heard that Dave had been arrested and had come to see what had transpired so far. As we came up the road past the compound we could see all the white BLM vehicles parked in the rest area alongside Interstate 15 just beyond the compound area in Toquop Wash. They had it all fenced off with orange plastic net fencing with Don't Stop signs. We took pictures as we drove by.

Just after we exited on the Bunkerville Exit 112 we came immediately upon more orange plastic net fencing enclosing an area about 200' by 200' with signs on it that read "First Amendment Area" and there was one gold suburban parked there with a man inside holding a sign. There were other signs that had been posted on the fence that said, "The 1st Amendment is Not an area." Since when was the First Amendment restricted to an Area? What a slap in the face to the Constitution and the American people! I also learned that there had been set up another such "Area" on the West End of Bunkerville and the rules had been posted that only 25 people at a time could occupy these areas and only occupy one of the areas at a time, dictated by Gayle Marrs-Smith, BLM Field Manager. That's how they uphold the Constitution?

(credit AP, dailymail.uk)

The 1st amendment states, "Congress shall make no laws...abridging the freedom of speech, freedom of the press, the right to peaceably assemble..."

I took pictures and then went over to the man and asked what he was doing? He said this was the First Amendment Area where we could protest for the Bundys. I asked him where everyone else was. He stated that they were down the road towards Bunkerville.

We drove on for another three miles until we came across the huge 50' poles that were being erected by a group of folks. They

(credit janbtucker.com)

(credit AP, dailymail.uk)

had set up a travel trailer and many cars with people and signs already posted on the chain link fence and picket signs walking up and down the roadway. They were trying to get the big sign hung up. We joined them and got out our signs, posting them on the fence and carrying them with us as we paraded up and down the roadside.

There was a sign posted on the fence about Dave Bundy being a political prisoner and gave a phone number for all to call for his release. Which many did!

There were about 50-60 people there and I noticed a couple of young men carrying side arms. I was curious and stepped up close behind them to try to catch a little of their conversation. One of them was a young black man who was in the military and from Las Vegas.

I believe that they were there just checking things out to see what this was really all about.

Cliven and David Bundy
(credit theblaze.com)

I also learned that Nevada was an "open carry" state for firearms. They do uphold the 2nd amendment so far.

We had been there for just a few hours when Cliven pulled in with Dave from Las Vegas. Dave was still in his clothing he was wearing in the attack on Sunday. I asked him if I could interview him to which he agreed and I recorded that interview live with many of his friends and family standing nearby.

You can watch that live on www.youtube.com. Just type Dave Bundy in the search bar. It is very touching. It was a very warm day in the Nevada desert even though it was still April. My friends had to get back home so I loaded them up and headed for home. I felt like I really needed to stay and support the Bundy Family because I also wanted to video Cliven and record his whole story and learn his reasoning behind the fees everybody kept getting hung up on.

As we headed home I again tried to take photos of the BLM compound on the top of the hill and the compound up Toquop Wash. After I returned everyone to their residence I headed back home with questions unanswered and couldn't sleep. Someone had mentioned that the signs going into the Utah Port of Entry had been covered up that says "All Livestock Must Stop." I wanted to check it out.

EPISODE TWO

❧

Unmarked Vehicles

I started out the next morning, Tuesday 7 April, for Bunkerville again. This time alone. I knew that if I wanted to get the information and photos I needed I would have to be on my own, free to roam and come and go as needed. On the way I noticed there were many, many chem trails in the skies. As I was driving I would often stop along the way and take pictures of them. As I drove past the Utah Port of Entry I stopped and took pictures of the signs that had been covered up with dark brown plastic and another covered in paper. The "All Livestock must stop" signs were in fact covered up.

Return to the Ranch

After I passed Mesquite I was watching for the BLM area and compound. I slowed up to about 65 mph and got in the right lane as close as I could to get the best pictures. There was a Blue Metro police car there with his lights on and I noticed a new black unmarked SUV pulled over there also. They were watching me as I drove by. In fact the one black SUV pulled out just behind me. I sped up and passed a diesel truck to put distance between us. As I turned right onto the Bunkerville Exit 112 I pulled off the road to stop and take pictures again of the First Amendment Area and some strange chem trails that were in a shape of a figure 8.

It was very odd indeed. While I was standing out of my truck on the running board the black unmarked SUV with dark tinted glass windows came off the exit and slowed down as it passed me. I got back in the truck and headed towards the ranch. A new looking light gray unmarked truck passed me on the road and stopped just ahead on the left of the road to meet up with the black SUV that had Colorado license plates. I took pictures as I passed and then again after they came down the road past the Check Point Area where I had stopped for a few minutes to get updates.

More Arrests

I pulled into the Bundy Ranch house about 8:30 am. Things were very busy there. Family members were coming and going with grandchildren and friends and relatives stopping by to check on the family. When I could finally get a few minutes alone with Cliven we went into the front yard by the big tree and I began our interview. We had been interviewing for no more than eight minutes when we were interrupted by someone who had to talk to Cliven on the phone. We began again and two minutes into it his youngest daughter came screaming out through the front door that "they" had Arden and Clancey down by the river! Not wanting to miss anything, I ran and jumped into my truck and headed for the river. As I came upon the crowd that had gathered there I accidentally dropped my strap in the road when I hopped out of my truck to take pictures

There were approximately a dozen white SUVs, gray trucks and black SUVs, along with the white trucks that were blocking the gravel roadway in front of the red pickup the boys were in. As I hurried back to the middle of the road to pick up my strap I noticed the men in uniforms sitting in the black SUV parked across the road. They were just sitting there watching.

Another silver SUV was parked in front of the situation with at least one man who looked like he had on a uniform just sitting there. I took pictures. I also took video footage of the men standing at each window of the pickup who were asking for the boys IDs. The boys gave them their driver licenses as many Bundy family members and even local people driving by stopped and joined in hollering at the men to leave the boys alone. One mother was even screaming, "Leave the little boys alone; take the old lady" (referring to herself as she held out her hands).

She continued, "You were all boys once and you all have families. What would your mothers think about what you are doing?" She even went so far as to say to one of them, "What are you doing here? You look like an Iraqi; I thought this was America!" Many more were hollering things like, "Go back where you came from," "They were just taking pictures," "Get off our public lands," "This is We the People's Land," and "How much do you get paid to harass unarmed American citizens?"

As the yelling escalated the two men standing at the red pickup were approached by another man and were told something about backing off. The agents handed back the driver license to the driver but simply tossed the other boy's license into the truck on the passenger side. They had to wait for the other three pickups to back out so they could leave. As they were backing out the protest gained momentum, with people realizing that they were winning with numbers! That was the answer! We needed lots of people so the agents would listen! They exclaimed how it felt so good like they had won back just a little bit of freedom in America at that instant.

As the agents drove off I took pictures of them and then got in my truck and headed back towards the ranch to finish my interview with Cliven. There were about six white SUVs directly in front of me and I was following them as they hit the dirt road on the left, leading up to Gold Butte Mountain. I watched as they pulled off to the left directly behind the hill and started circling the wagons in a giant dust bowl. Again I stopped and took pictures. It was as if they were a bunch of bees lying in wait to light upon the next victim. It was eerie.

Documentation

As I approached the ranch house, Cliven was still there and family members were already on their cell phones with those that were at the scene getting all the details. I think everyone had cell phones and cameras which are great weapons for providing proof. One daughter, Bailey, was uploading all the video and images from everyone's electronic devices and had already begun the Bundyranch.blogspot.com website. The internet was going wild.

What caused all the ruckus was that one of the older Bundy relatives was down along the road when he noticed a white helicopter trying to herd the cattle along the river. He didn't have a camera but did have a cell phone and called for someone to come with a camera and get pictures. The cattle were being driven and the poor little calves couldn't keep up with their mothers, so they were being left in the underbrush hiding or trying to run to keep up, but would stumble and fall as the helicopters would keep pushing them, even hitting them with their landing runners! That's why the boys went down and others followed to get pictures.

Cliven never got involved with any of these things. In fact he instructed his whole family: "Be peaceful and not threatening because how could they be guilty of crimes they did not yet commit? Just let them do their evil deeds and the Lord will tell us when to stand up."

For many of them it was very difficult to watch the nasty deeds that were taking place in front of them. They would gather together periodically and talk about the things that had been transpiring the past few days.

In the house things were really crazy. Computers and laptops covered the Kitchen table. The one phone they had was ringing off the wall. Whoever was closest would pick it up and I listened to some of them giving answers that contradicted each other. There was mass confusion about the Face Book page and the email. After listening to one of the children get upset and yell and then slam down the phone I realized they needed a PR person and I needed to be it!

I was unrelated and unattached! I had been through this all before during the experience with the Grand Staircase Escalante National Monument. I knew how devious the media are and how they twist stories to fit their own agendas. They may be friendly to your face, but they write very harsh and critical stories against you. I knew the ones who told the truth and tried to represent the truth even at their own cost. I understand the issues at hand and the agenda of the United Nations. This is an innocent and loving family. Trusting, truthful, honest and God fearing! A Family that sticks together even when they have their own differences. They follow the Patriarch and honor and respect their women. They are real cowboys of the West who work hard and expect nothing less from their own children and grandchildren and those around them. They have compassion and love for everyone. Anyone who walks through their door is treated like family and invited to eat a meal or refreshments. They live very modestly and don't have all the fancy and frilly latest clothing and vehicles.

The kitchen table was turned into our office. We pulled the pictures and everything off the dining room walls so we could turn it into bulletin boards for information. We began to formulate an organization plan. There were many calls from the media and we didn't want any of the news outlets to be ignored. We wanted the true story out and they all wanted to talk to Cliven. He was already going hoarse as he had been talking non-stop for the past few days. We had to make a plan.

A Plan

The Family would meet together very early each morning and have breakfast and family prayer.

Each would be delegated an area of responsibility. To ease the pressure of the media we decided to have a Daily Press Conference up at the Check Point Area at 1 p.m. There were still a lot of media we had to schedule independently because they were from all over the US and 52 other countries who had live shows and couldn't travel this far. It was brutal as I would limit the amount of time each one could speak with Cliven. I began to insert some of his older sons and then even some of the daughters in his place.

As I would receive the incoming calls I would write down the callers' names, numbers and messages. There was just no time to act upon everything that was coming in. I had never been able to finish my interview with Cliven about the fees but I did know that the BLM had stated that on Monday he owed $300,000 in back fees for the past 20 years. On Wednesday they stated it was over $1,000,000 and by Friday it was raised to $10,000,000. Now that's Inflation!

Some Historical Perspective

After all the phone calls from all the people across the country we had some of the old ranchers who had been pushed off the land also sending information about their side of the story. How they had been abused and driven off their land. Many, many stories from all over the country how the Federal Bureaucrats had stolen their homes, their mines, their money, their ranches, their lands and the stories kept coming and coming. As I began to piece together the real situation here I began to realize what had happened. I came to the following conclusion:

In 1864 Nevada became a State. In 1877 Cliven's Maternal Grandmother settled this ranch and it had been in the family ever since and Cliven had even purchased more personal property to make it the 150 acre ranch it is today.

In 1930 the Federal Government established a Bureau of Land Management because there were so many people running cattle and sheep on these open state lands that they needed some kind of management. Those that already used the land were being charged so much per head of livestock that they were grazing on that land. There was lots of open range land. This range land was 95 square miles with 30 miles of the Virgin River running through it. As far as you can see in 360 degree radius. Ninety percent of the land in Nevada was not privately owned.

Everything went smoothly for years and every rancher paid their AUM's (which stands for animal per unit) until 1993 when the BLM changed their contracts. The EPA (Environmental Protection Agency) came out with a new ruling called the ESA (Endangered Species Act) which listed the desert tortoise as an endangered species. The desert tortoise was very plentiful around Bunkerville and the Nevada Deserts. But the agency decided they would build a refuge by Las Vegas and gather up the tortoises and protect them there.

The truth of the matter was that scientific studies showed that the Desert Tortoise in fact was thriving because they actually feed on the cattle and sheep dung. The fact is that today in the refuge outside of Las Vegas they now have so many Desert Tortoise that they have to euthanize them from lack of funding. Good job EPA!? (http://rt.com/usa/desert-tortoises-euthanize-nevada-024/)

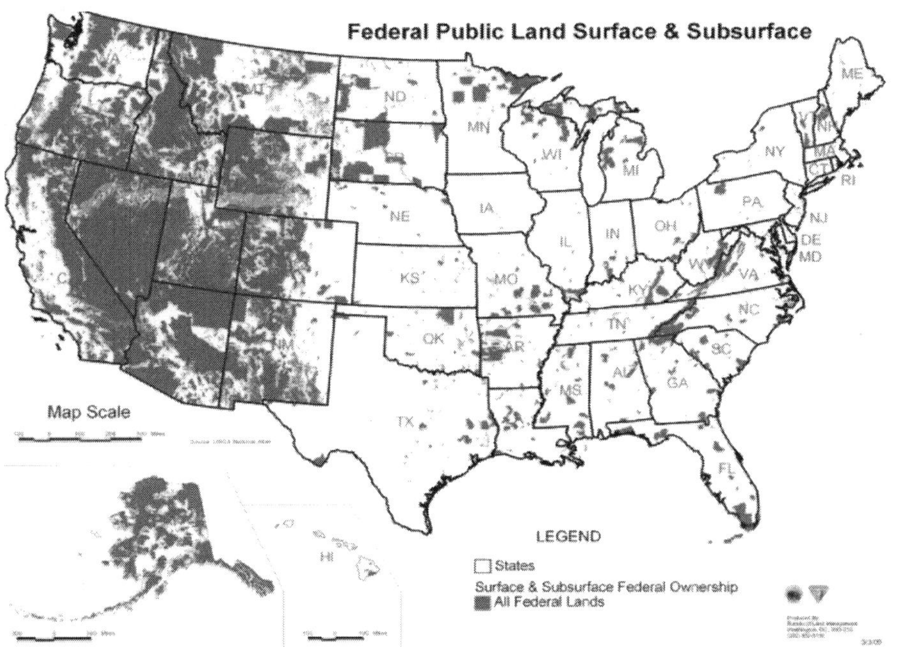

The Federal Government owns 52 percent of the land in Western states, according to data compiled by the Congressional Research Service *(credit Bureau of Land Management)*

Who are the true environmentalists? The ranchers, farmers, timber industries and many others who make their living off the land are the true environmentalists. If they don't care for the land and wildlife they in turn cannot make a living. If you don't weed your garden it is taken over by the weeds. Thus because there are these so called environmental groups who solicit many people to support them through incorrect media and information end up destroying the land in which they profess to be protecting. The forests are overgrown and left as giant fire hazards and even too overgrown for the wildlife. Endangered Species Act is only a vice and an excuse to control the land.

In 1993 the new contract with the 53 ranchers in Clark County was changed to say that the ranchers had to deplete their cattle to

150 head and then allow the BLM to come and re-implement any new rules they felt like any time they wanted. This was just an open door to turn all the ranchers into willing sellers as they couldn't even make a living on their ranches now. It would never be profitable!

That is exactly what happened and the only rancher smart enough not to sign such an agreement was Cliven Bundy. He stated that nobody in their right mind would sign a contract of such a nature. I later discovered that some of the other ranchers were beaten down and none of their children wanted to continue ranching when you can't make money. (So America, I ask you, "Where do you get your beef from?") Those ranchers that tried to hold out were even offered to have their wells purchased at $1,000,000 each. If they had a couple or three wells on their land that was a small fortune to them and they sold out!

Grazing Fees

Cliven did not feel right about not paying any fees, but when he saw all his friends and ranchers were paying, he made out his check in 1993 to Clark County because he said he had no contract with the BLM or Federal Government to manage his land. He paid the check to Clark County and they accepted it. When he went again to pay his fees they refused to accept them and tried to give him a check for the fees he had paid previously. Cliven never did cash that check, so they still have that money.

The strange thing is, in 1994 the BLM declared that area as "Non Grazing," which would mean that Cliven would not only not be assessed for AUM's but also that the law would have to revert back to the Taylor Grazing Act of 1934 that states that in an "Open Range" area, if you don't want cattle on your property then you must "Fence Them Out!"

The Taylor Grazing Act for the State of Nevada says, NRS 568.230: "It is unlawful ... (to) restrict or interfere with the customary use of the land for grazing livestock by any person who, by himself or herself or the person's grantors or predecessors, has become established, under and in accordance with the customs of the grazers of the region involved."

Specifics of the Law

What does customary mean? NRS 568.240 states: "Customary or established use...to include the continuous, open, notorious, peaceable and public use of such range seasonally for a period of 5 years or longer immediately before March 30, 1931, by the person or the person's grantors or predecessors in interest,...Any change in customary use so established must not be made after March 30, 1931, so as to prevent, restrict or interfere with the customary or established use of any other person or persons. NRS 568.230 to 568-290, "...does not prohibit any such established user from continuing his or her grazing use, as established by operation of law or in accordance with such customs." NRS 568.290 states: "Nothing in NRS 568.230 to 568.290, inclusive, amends or repeals existing law regarding the grazing use of the public lands or of water for the purpose or watering livestock, or modifies or compromises any valid rights or priorities which exist therein on March 30, 1931."

The law clearly states that if there is no legal fence, there can be no trespass damages claimed.

NRS 569.440 (b) "If any owner or occupier of any grounds or crops trespassed upon by livestock...whether enclosed by a legal fence or not, kills, maims or materially injures the livestock so trespassing, the owner or occupier of the grounds or crops is liable to the owner of the livestock for all damages..."

Therefore the BLM knew their own law and could not charge AUM's nor could they charge him for trespass because they had failed to build any fences. There is also in Nevada what is called "preemptive law" or in some states it is known as "prescriptive law" or "adverse possession." If someone decides to squat on your land or at your house or on your property of any kind, if you do not have an agreement, or contract with them and they pay you nothing even though you know about it, then after a number of years it becomes their personal property. In Nevada that time limit is five years.

How long has Cliven been on this property? At least 60 years!

The Crux of the Issue

The real issue is whose land is this—Nevada State Public Land or Federal Lands? Can the Federal Government own land according to the Constitution? (Article 1 sec. 8)

Article X of the Constitution says: "The powers not delegated to the United States by the Constitution, nor prohibited by it to the States, are reserved to the States respectively, or to the people.

The Bureau of Land Management is just that, a Management Company hired to do a job, not to own the land it manages. We have just become indoctrinated to say "Federal Lands or BLM Land" which in fact it is not!!! That is where this fight begins. Cliven is the last rancher standing.

I had been trying to explain this to others as fast as I could but I was still at the ranch attached to the phone and desk.

American Lands Council

There is a group called the American Lands Council (ALC) headed up by Ken Ivory, Doug Heaton, and a few other brave men. They have been working hard to get the Western States together to declare their Sovereignty and to demand that Congress honor their Constitutional promise to be admitted into the Union on the same "Equal Footing" as all of the original 13 colonies were and as all of the other states have been!

This promise is the Enabling Act—*"An Act to enable the people of Nevada to form a Constitution and State Government, and for the admission of such State into the Union on equal footing with the original States"*—signed by President Abraham Lincoln and Secretary of State William H. Seward. There are 11 Western States that have still never had their unappropriated lands released back to them by the Federal Government as they have been promised to do so. If you research the history of this nation you will see that the Federal Government had Federal Claims on the western lands to the Mississippi river in 1774 and extended that to the Western Territories as acquired.

It is crucial that the Congress dispose of these lands to the Western States which will be a great economic relief to the Budget of the Federal Government and the whole United States. They will no longer have to subsidize these unappropriated lands getting nothing in return for the billions of dollars spent on them every year. All the other States have had to have their Statehood promises granted also. It is *very important* that we do this immediately as the United States is in a dire financial crises now! Get your congressmen to adhere to their obligation to these states immediately. Senators and Representatives must be stopped from selling these State Lands to other countries for their personal gain!

I felt like they would be great champions in this fight for sovereignty because that is their main focus! I knew that if I could get the media, here at the ranch, to catch the vision then they would grab hold of the ALC and understand more of the overreach of this Federal Government!

My goal has always been to get the right people connected to the people of the same mindset in order to get the strength to further these actions. There are many people that believe the same and are fighting their own little battles that really take big numbers of people to make the difference. We must gather together!

A Clear Indictment

One of the calls I also received was from a gentleman down in Search Light, Nevada who worked with the Wildlife Fish and Game. He stated that for the past 10 plus years there have been over 300 head of feral cattle running wild down there. Feral cattle, for those who don't know, are cattle that are wild and unclaimed by anyone. They are not branded nor inspected and become the ward of the state when left unattended. The herd had grown so large that they were creating a dangerous nuisance. They can attack people and property. The Wildlife Fish and Game had repeatedly begged the BLM to come in and get rid of these cattle. The report was always the same, "We can't; we don't have enough money and resources to do it."

This gentleman had gathered a number of local cowboys together five years ago and they were able to round up about 30-50 head and took them to the livestock auction but because they were feral and had not received inspections and vaccinations they could not be sold for human consumption and therefore brought a very low price. The State received the money but said it wasn't worth the cost to have them rounded up and sold. So the BLM has done nothing about them. The same situation has been a huge problem with wild horses around Reno, Nevada, and wild horses in Iron County, Utah etc. We begin to see there are many of these same issues all over the different areas of the United States and they can all be traced back to failure of the BLM.

Wild Horses Issue

There are wild horses in Iron County, Utah that are causing major damage to the land and other animals that aren't being managed by the BLM. Commissioner Dave Miller reported that the BLM who was supposed to be managing the horses said they told him that they have no money to take care of them. The BLM told me that because of the environmental groups that have pressured new laws to be put in place which prohibits them from killing any horses, they can only adopt them out or catch them and pay for their maintenance themselves, due to the lack of interested parties to adopt them. It is just way too expensive to manage them. All of the BLM employees are not bad. We just have some power hungry monsters. They are the ones who are way out of control!

A Catalog of Federal Abuses

We compiled a large list of abuses of federal agencies as calls continued to come in. I heard stories and captured the names and numbers of dozens of people willing to testify of these things.

Sample List of Claimants

- Bill Jordan from Reno, Nevada, told me he had two properties taken by Harry Reid in 1983: Goosbrry Mine and Calaposa Mine property in Lawrenceville. *(www.Gooseberryfrauds.com)*
- Benjamin Miller of Miller Machine & Oils had a mineral patent in the Black Hills of South Dakota. He has pictures of his Grandmother who was raised on the property. His Grandpa Jackson filed a Deed on mineral rights that was on a military post but privately owned. The land was in the shape of a J. It had been sold 11 times but with the help of an Archeologist Benjamin was able to locate the property. It was uncovered that in 1904 the Government had been claiming all mineral rights in all states. But the South Dakota Supreme Court removed the Senior Judge Delaney in 7 months and retired Judge Fuller who were part of the land grab of "Privately owned property in exclusive Federal Legislature Jurisdiction."

- Chris, Active Army, told me his Ivan Family Ranch in Reno, Nevada was forced out of the Cattle Business.
- Matt Klump—his Family had cattle impounded and stolen in Graham County, Arizona and his uncle Wally spent 1 year in prison from 1992-1993. (Even while Sheriff Richard Mack was the Sheriff there.)
- Raymond Yowell had Cattle taken.
- Randy and Laura Weaver had their Land stolen by the Federal Government in Montana.
- Coral Silvey had land taken in Kansas.
- Judith Gibson of South Lake, Tahoe, California had land taken 16 years ago.
- 2007 —The House of Representatives passed a carbon tax by the vote of 85 Legislatures that lets them steal property from American Citizens.
- Don Alt in Silver Springs, Nevada, had $40,000 worth of damage done to his range. He was forced to reduce his cattle herd to 30 cows.
- Dalton Wilson of Reno, Nevada said Judge Sandovall, without a jury trial, ordered the BLM to tear down his house and barn.

Salazar's successor, Sally Jewell, is not only pressing forward with redundant hydraulic fracturing rules, but is threatening the West with the use of President Obama's power, under the Antiquities Act of 1906, to prevent economic activity with massive national-monument designations. This was a tactic of the War on the West that President Clinton had already started—just like our Grand Staircase Escalante Monument closed now to economic activity, including what might have become the world's largest high-quality, low-sulfur coal mine.

Now Jewel has signed off on a decision by the EPA to put a million acres of Wyoming land—including the entire town of Riverton, Wyoming with a population of over 10,000—into the Windy River Indian Reservation, despite the indisputable historical fact this land was ceded to the U.S. in a 1904 agreement between the tribes, and in opposition to a unanimous 1998 U.S. Supreme Court ruling regarding a comparable situation in South Dakota.

It is difficult to exaggerate the quasi-religious zeal with which the War on the West is waged.

The list goes on, but maybe you know of others yourselves.

Individuals feel so abused by this tyrannical Government and they are singled out with very little support from other friends and neighbors. We have all been so indoctrinated that we are afraid to speak up; and if it doesn't affect us personally then we turn our heads away, breathing a sigh of relief that it wasn't us. Please people—Wake Up!

Misinformation

Misinformation was another problem that we were facing that day in trying to discover where the BLM might be taking the cattle to sell. We knew that they were contracted to sell them at the "R" Livestock Auction in Monroe, Utah, but due to the phone calls from people who were upset with the auction, had shown up and picketed the Wednesday auction the week before to let buyers know that it would be a bad move to buy stolen cattle from this auction house.

There were reports calling in that someone saw trailers full of cattle being taken to Colorado, through Nevada, through Utah and even to California. There were reports that a local trucker had been offered good money to haul a load of cattle from the compound. He refused!

We even received a copy of a contract from a special friend that had been found with an auction house in California. We contacted the auction house and sent a letter of warning. They turned down the contract, I suppose, because no cattle were sent there either. We just didn't know how many they had actually hauled out.

Santilli Reporting

That evening I was talking to a young reporter from Guerrilla Media out of California by the name of Pete Santilli, an ex-marine. We were very impressed with his reporting and the stand he was taking. He was truly interested in what was happening out here and wanted to see it for himself. He explained to me about 8 p.m. that he was closing down his studio as we were speaking and he was loading up his car and on his way to the Ranch. "People need to know about this!" he exclaimed.

At this point we had some self-appointed bodyguards show up who wanted to step in and protect the family. They began to organize and set up their points of operation. We didn't know where they came from and had never asked anyone to do such a thing. They just said it was their Constitutional duty and began to encourage people to come to the ranch. We had already invited everyone to come, barring none. This is America and these are State public lands. We needed support and the more people, the stronger the statement. These guardians had learned that we actually had snipers with guns pointing at us continually. There were motion detectors and night ops, surveillance cameras and coverage everywhere.

Pete Santilli
(credit Americans for Legal Immigration PAC)

We got to sleep about midnight that night. About 4:00 a.m. I received a phone call from Santilli asking for directions. He told me he was about an hour away and was still coming. I loaded up and had to head out by 5 o'clock AM to make it to the Monroe auction by 8:00 that morning. We had a group there to protest the auction and I wanted to take pictures if there were actually any Bundy cattle there. Pete called a few times and I didn't dare wait for him because I had a long way to go. I missed him by about 10 minutes I guess. He asked me to take pictures and let him know how many cattle and protestors were there.

When I arrived at Monroe at the "R" Livestock Auction there were already a half a dozen vehicles set up with signs and men wandering around. I parked my truck and proceeded to set up my flags and signs. Some of the local people were stopping in also. One man went inside to talk to the owner and ask him why he was doing this. His answer was, "I have a right to make a living also!" He was very upset with all the picketing going on! Other men went and checked to see if any of the Bundy cattle were there. They were not! Bundys have their own breed of cattle—a Brahma cross—because they are developed to withstand the hot dry climate of

Bundy Ranch cattle

the Nevada deserts and they have never eaten hay in their lives. They live off of browse (dry brush that looks like weeds) and grasses, and yet they thrive on it.

Ryan Bundy, wife, and son

We had Ryan Bundy and his wife and little children there also carrying signs. There were families, men, women, children, cowboys and businessmen. It was a great turnout and many people passing by honked in support! The auction was still going on that morning but it was very small. We held a little program and sang songs and even happy birthday to two year-old Moroni Bundy. We had a beautiful prayer offered. About noon some of us had to leave and I loaded up and headed back to Nevada.

Miscarriage of Justice

We had the local sheriff department drive by making sure nothing got out of hand, but of course it didn't because this was just a peaceful protest. We were feeling sorry for the owner but he had made a very bad business decision and we had to stop these kinds of actions. You must draw a line in the sand if you are ever going to stand up against evil. The BLM had no right to sell the cattle. They only had a Federal Court order to remove them from the land, which was illegal as Cliven had never been to Federal Court. He was trying to keep it in the State Courts but the Federal Judges took it upon themselves to make it a Federal Case and made the decisions without even a trial. Where do they get that authority?

Dr. Larry R. Moses commented: "The federal court that ruled Mr. Bundy had to remove his cattle refused to consider this federal law. It was another case of a federal agency picking and choosing which law to follow and which to ignore. One must ask Senator Reid if this is a law that he believes should be obeyed, or is the law as the regular citizen who ignores the law? Again I must tell you I am not a lawyer but I can read and this is pretty clear that customary rights exist here, since the Bundy's meet the requirements of NRS 568.240. Harry Reid is a graduate of Las Vegas High School and I am sure they taught him how to read.

The federal courts ignored state law when they ruled against rancher Cliven Bundy and found in favor of the Federal Government. The facts are, the courts have ordered Mr. Bundy, on more than one occasion, to remove his cattle and he has refused to do so.

When the BLM threatened a Nye County rancher with the same fate as Mr. Bundy, he also took them to court. The difference in the two cases is that the courts found in favor of that rancher. Based on these court decisions, the local sheriff stood by his side. The Sheriff of Clark County has been criticized for not taking a similar stand. However, to do so he would have to obstruct a federal court order. No right thinking law enforcement agent would do that. The Clark County Sheriff did the best he could by refusing to get involved. The courts awarded the Nye County rancher 14 million dollars in damages. The BLM, the same agency that has attacked Mr. Bundy for not abiding by the court's decisions, refused to honor the judgment. They have appealed to the Ninth Circuit Court. One federal official has been quoted to say, "We will win there; this is our court."

On my return ride to the Ranch I received a phone call from people calling in to check on us. I was told they were watching the live streaming on the internet of an attack that was going on at the Ranch. I called the Ranch House to see what was happening.

Encounter with Agent in Charge

I learned that while I was at the Auction, Reporter Pete Santilli had been interviewing people around the ranch and also had gone to the BLM encampment just off the freeway. He had requested a meeting with whomever was in charge. He and a fellow reporter were met by the "Special Agent in Charge," a man by the name of Daniel P. Love. Santilli tried to be the mediator between the Bundy's and the agents. He was informed that the agents had been sent to confiscate the cattle and he was prepared to do just that. Santilli asked Dan if 10,000 unarmed Americans showed up to back up the Bundy's would he back down? Dan told Santilli in no uncertain terms, "You better hope 10,000 people show up because with the number you have now, that ain't gonna happen!"

Daniel Love
(credit guerillamedianetwork.com)

Santilli pressed further and said, "You would shoot unarmed Americans to save cattle?" Dan told Santilli, "We are talking about cattle! And don't you do one thing, and I mean it, not one thing to interfere or you will answer to me! Got It?!" "You now have my cell number and you can call me if you have questions." Then he asked, "Is that perfectly clear?" You can listen to the whole conversation in the Archives of www.guerillamedia.com under Pete Santilli. Search Bundy Ranch.

Backhoe Battle

The group of citizens and family members, along with media were at the check point area after Santilli returned and were eating lunch when they noticed a caravan of the White SUVs coming down the Gold Butte Mountain headed for the highway. The caravan was different this time. Instead of trucks pulling horse trailers they had a huge dump truck pulling a flatbed trailer with a backhoe on it, in the center of the caravan. The family members that saw this started to get upset. Why did they need a dump truck and backhoe to gather cattle? Were they killing the cattle and burying them? Some of the people ran, others drove across the bridge to meet the caravan. They wanted to stop them and see what was in that dump truck?

They arrived just before the caravan hit the pavement and the crowd tried to stop them. Pete Santilli raised his index finger to signal the driver to stop while the others around him all started hollering and running towards the vehicles. They wanted to find out if in fact there were criminal actions going on. It was obvious that they had no intention of stopping. After the first white vehicles came onto the road, they had to slow down because of all the 40-50 people there.

Ammon Bundy was riding his 4-wheeler and saw that the dump truck was not stopping. Ammon pulled his 4-wheeler in front of the truck and bailed off just before the truck plowed into it. Ammon raced to the top of the dirt plateau to try and see what was inside the truck but the hill wasn't high enough. He raced back down where two of Cliven's sisters were trying to climb on the back of the truck to get pictures of what it was carrying. They did get pictures. It was pipes and scraps from one of their water systems.

At the same time another sister, Margaret was running toward the vehicles shouting and trying to get them to stop. The SUVs had stopped and agents jumped out with guns, tasers, and dogs. Everyone had cell phones and cameras! Santilli was streaming live on the internet as one of the agents runs up behind Margaret, throws his arms around her, picks her up and hip chucks her to the ground. The agent was young and weighed about 260 lbs. compared to Margaret who is 57 years- old and about 140 lbs. She never saw him coming and the attack caught her by surprise. She skinned her hand and knee which also left bruises and scrapes on her arms, knee and leg.

When Ammon saw his aunt being thrown to the ground he immediately turned toward her and, with his hands wide open and arms outstretched, started yelling at the agents. "Why did you do that? She is a mother, a grandmother, a three-time survivor of cancer. They almost lost her to cancer again just last year."

The agent who had just thrown her down had a taser in his left hand and reached up and tased Ammon in the neck and chest. Ammon turned away quickly to his right and said it was all he could do to control his shaking hand to reach across and rip the wires and hooks from his body. When he turned again toward the agents, another one tased him and sicced the dog on him at the same time. The taser hit him in the front of his left shoulder about the time the dog attacked. As he whirled around, he kicked the dog, which ran back to hide behind the agent. A woman and a man who were there started grabbing for the wires. As the woman reached for them, they arced across her arm, leaving burn marks—even though they were able to pull the wires free to stop the 50,000 volts being injected into Ammon. A third taser that was fired and hit Ammon in the arm and chest. By now the crowd had it down and they quickly yanked the wires free.

Confrontation leading to taser attacks
(credit freedominourtime.com)

The youngest Bundy daughter—Stetsy, who was pregnant—was threatened with a dog attack. People began to call 911 for help. There was no response! Santilli called 911 and an operator answered and instructed them to "Stop Calling! You are tying up our lines!"

Everyone was yelling, taking pictures and Santilli's video was live streaming through Guerrilla Media. It went viral. They say it was the fastest viewed video ever. There were 15,000,000 views in just a short time. The whole nation had witnessed this! There was even a police car that drove by but didn't stop.

Gayle Marrs-Smith, BLM Field Manager, is the person who made the decree to close off all the roads and trails, thus leaving the city of Mesquite and the townships of Bunkerville, Logandale, and Overton isolated from the rest of the State. Logandale and Overton citizens could only access State Highway 169 and Bunkerville could not even drive on State Highway 170 because it was being patrolled by federal agents with guns, tasers, and dogs. All other roads had been closed and if you drove on them you would either get a ticket or even be arrested by federal agents!

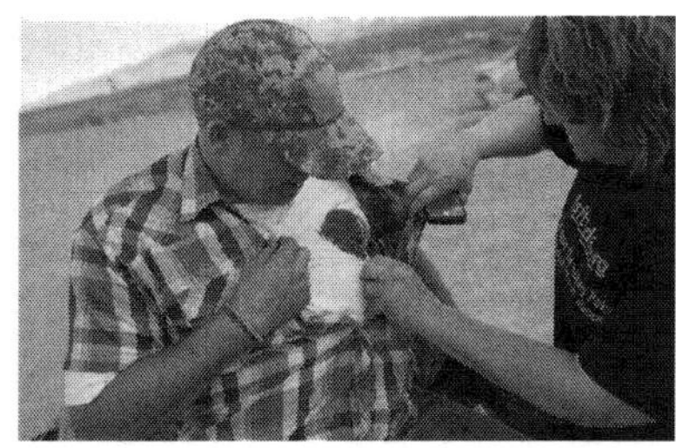

Ammon Bundy's taser wound
(credit theepochtimes.com)

If the Federal Government is not subject to state law within public lands, does that mean that over 80% of the state of Nevada is not really a state? Why do the citizens have to obey State laws then? So I ask you again, is Nevada a State or a Territory being ruled by a dictatorship?

I arrived just after they gathered at the Check Point Area. A nurse in plain clothing was there trying to check on Ammon and Margaret. We were all taking pictures and asking questions. There were knots as big as half dollars all raised up on Ammon's neck and on his arm. I took pictures of the bloody spots on his t-shirt. Later I took photos of the taser wires and barbs that were found alongside the road where Ammon had been tased.

A Dilemma

Sheriff Gillespie of Clark County was refusing to provide the protection he was called upon to give. It seems as though the Sheriff was now under the power of the Federal Government instead of the people. We elect Sheriffs to protect us from such tyranny and yet the Clark County Sheriff Gillespie would not even show up or send any help from the sheriff's department. Not only is he the Sheriff in Clark County but he is also the head of the Las Vegas Metro Police Department. It was obvious he had no intentions of helping.

When that happens to US Citizens then the Constitution allows and demands that the people form a Militia for protection. That is exactly what happened. In accordance with this Constitutional principle, almost as if governed by some unseen hand, Militia groups began to call from all over the US asking if we wanted them to come. We said that we weren't asking them to come because we couldn't be responsible for them but everyone was welcome and they should do what they felt was right.

Every morning and every evening we would always pray for protection and it was amazing to see how the hearts of the people were being touched across the whole country. One group after the other would call from the different states. They began to pour in. Driving, carpooling, hitch hiking and some even walking for miles.

I recall being at the Check Point area when I heard the blowing of shofars. Col. Ray Potter and his friend Rand with his son Nick had received information about the troubles at the Ranch. Rand told Pete Santilli in an interview later that he had been learning about "Judaism" that corresponded to his beliefs. He said with two witnesses present you need to pay attention. He woke up with a feeling to go see the Bundys. He called his son and Col. Potter and explained that the Blood Moon was going to pass over in a couple of days and the ranch was right in the center of its visibility. He also said it was important to follow their promptings of the Spirit and that they needed to go pray at the Virgin River and perform a Shofar Ceremony.

Rand blowing his Kudo horn

The Shofar is a Kudo horn of an African kudo antelope. Kudo is the "Trump of God." It was blown by Charlton Heston in the film "The Ten Commandments," conveying *you must come hither when you hear the trump of God, for there is an enemy with a sword in the land.* The Kudo horn has been used in Israel for centuries. In Hebrew, Kudo means "Glory to God." The frequency is a sacred Kabala or Flower of Light of Creation, and can be heard thousands of miles above the earth. Col. Potter offers the prayer in Hebrew. They came to invoke the blessings of Heaven.

There has been a controversy over the right to have a militia. There appear to be justifiable reasons for today's militia to exist. The Constitution and the Second Amendment are cited and, under certain conditions, a militia may well be valid. If, for instance, the Federal Government suddenly grabbed all power, and declared itself sovereign and abolished the citizens' right to vote (how about voter fraud?), a situation would exist whereby tyranny as understood by reasonable men would exist; at that moment the citizen militia as envisioned by the Founding Fathers would be rightly formed. As citizens and militia, they could then justifiably fight to restore the Constitution of the United States. The armed citizen was the army that fought for the United States. Thus the citizen militia cannot be by definition the National Guard of today. This is too well understood to elaborate.

The major media could no longer ignore us. The phone had gone crazy! As I would be speaking to one person and I would get beeped at least 4 to 5 times on a call. I know there were a lot who wanted to contact us but just couldn't get in. I'm sorry for that. They were concerned people who were calling to encourage us and to tell their own stories of the nightmares they too have had to live through in similar situations.

The media were relentless! I tried to send them all to the daily press conferences we were holding at the Check Point Area at 1:00 p.m. That helped some.

Check Point Area

People were calling and coming with donations to help out. They brought food, money, supplies, clothing, sleeping bags, tents, books, legal help and information, so many things I can't number them all. We felt so grateful to all those that were sacrificing so much. It was unbelievable!

One precious little lady said she wanted to buy breakfast for everybody. She said she would not waste her money on ObamaCare but instead use the money to buy breakfast for everyone. She wished she could come but physically she was unable. There were many in that shape who wanted to help but couldn't. They all sent their prayers and, believe me, we felt them!

EPISODE THREE

Easter Weekend

With so many different sightings of people reporting that they saw Bundy cattle being transported across the country we began to wonder just how many cattle they actually had gathered and I didn't know if they could tell if any had been shipped or not.

Aerial Surveillance

I called one of my friends who had a plane. I asked if he would check to see if there was a "No Fly Zone" over that area. The report came back. There were no "No Fly Zones" anywhere near there. I had overheard someone say that they had rented a car and driven out because of a restricted "No Fly Zone." I explained what I was trying to do and asked if they would mind flying me early the next morning. "Absolutely" was the response. I wrapped up a few more interviews and headed for home late that evening.

It was early the next morning we boarded the plane. We did take a gun or two, just in case they tried to shoot us down. The sun had only been up for a short time when we came across the plateau overlooking the compound. There was only one spotter in his white truck on the ridge. He watched us through his rifle scope. Soon there were two or three more trucks en route to the top of the plateau as we circled overhead. We circled lower and lower so I could get some good photos of the corrals and cattle.

The caravan of trucks and trailers were just lining up to pull out. We flew across the open desert where there were trucks and agent vehicles posted in twos. They were all watching us through binoculars and scopes. After we made the 10th swoop over them we decided to head towards the river and ranch. When we approached the ranch we could see the men mounting their horses. We swooped over them a few times and took pictures of the ranch and the whole area. You could see how well manicured the land was when it is being managed by the ranchers compared to the dry and desolate desert. It was like an oasis in the desert. I waved but no one seemed to know it was me. I called on the phone but no one answered. I think everyone was outside trying to figure out who we were.

More Intelligence

Back on the road, I headed to the ranch. When I arrived, there were a couple of my old friends there who had just returned from flying over the compound and the ranch! What! We had the same idea and didn't even know it. With all of our pictures we were able to count how many head of cattle were in each corral. We had great pictures! They told me that as they were flying along the river that they had come upon two white helicopters that were pushing the cattle up the river. When the helicopters spotted their plane they actually chased them and tried to knock them out of the sky! WOW!

(credit AP, dailymail.uk)

Later that afternoon we were holding a press conference and had asked some public officials to show up. Michelle Fiorre, a Nevada Assembly Woman, and Representative Dean Heller were the two main ones who showed up! We were in the middle of the meeting and they were saying how they were in support of our cause when we got a telephone call that there was a group of protesters at Overton Beach that was being attacked by the agents. We heard that there were three young men that had been arrested and beaten. Ryan made the challenge to the State Officials that if they really wanted to show their support that they would travel with us right now to go help the people that were being attacked. We all jumped into our vehicles and took off in a caravan headed for Overton Beach.

During this time the County Fair was in full swing in Overton. It is a really big annual deal with Clark County. In fact the youngest son Arden was out to show one of his calves. It should really bring a pretty penny this year! Part of the family was really involved in activities with the fair. We traveled past the town and on to Overton Beach. The caravan of agents and trailers were gone by the time we arrived. There were still people there who had witnessed and videoed the things that went down there. One of the boys had not been arrested. One of the brothers had been beaten up, arrested and then released in the desert. The other brother had been beaten, arrested and hauled off somewhere near the Valley of Fire before he was set free. I guess the agents had decided that it did no good to take them to jail after Dave's publicity. We got some copies of the trouble and on one of the videos a young woman was asking the agents why they needed so many armed vehicles to protect three cattle trailers that were only carrying three cows. His answer was, "Because we were attacked by that woman yesterday [meaning Margaret] and they were throwing rocks at us." ***All lies!!!***

Video

After chasing down the wrong road trying to catch up with them, we turned around and met the media representatives who had stopped to interview one of the boys alongside the road who had been beaten up and arrested, then released. I took pictures and videos also. His face and head had the exact same red marks on the one side—where they had knelt on his head and stepped on him—and gravel marks on the opposite side of his face—just like Dave Bundy's. The boys said that they had crossed the *imaginary line* in the sand. They refused to move when they were ordered to disperse even though they were not armed or standing in the way of the caravan. They were just on the side of the dirt road. The politicians never did show up there, or we never saw them. Infowars was there reporting along with another Fox reporter in their motor home.

The next morning I received a call from my friends who had flown over the compound. They asked me who my pilot was. I told them I wasn't going to tell them, why? Apparently the FBI had contacted their pilot and was trying to scare them. They were threatening to pull their FCC License and put them out of business. They just wondered if we had the same problem. I said I didn't know but would have to check. I guess after our flight had stirred up the hornet's nest, the agents had copied down the tail numbers of the second plane. My pilot had not heard a thing. He said if they show up at the door, well, "It's nice knowin' ya!"

The BLM no-fly zone targets new helicopters from covering the story *(credit infowars.com)*

I had it checked out and, sure enough, they had now put up a "No Fly Zone" right over the compound.

That was really fast. It is a hard thing to get done and takes a long time usually. Red Tape ya' know, unless you have some great Government pull?

<u>Brian Johnson Text</u> (April 11 · Edited)

OMG!!! I must have ticked these guys off!!! Now there is a TFR over the Area. LOL!!! I love it!!! See that little red dot over there by southern Nevada, and todays date April 11!!!

<u>Sean Hannity Reporters</u>

When we got a call later that afternoon from the Sean Hannity Show with Fox News, they said they would like to pick up Cliven and drive around the ranch for a few hours and get pictures. I said, "I have a better idea, why don't you fly!" To my surprise they said OK and hired a helicopter for the next morning. I figured if they couldn't they would soon find out, plus they might have more influence than we do.

So Friday Morning April 11th amid all the phone calls and media we had a helicopter land in the yard as Cliven and one of his body guards were met and took a little news reporting flight for a few hours.

Amidst all the chaos in the house—with people coming and going, interviews and phone calls—we managed to get a phone call in to Sheriff Gillespie's office. Cliven told him that "We the People" would like to talk to him tomorrow morning at our Check Point Area, that we had some very important messages for him, and that the media would all be there to get his response. Cliven also faxed a letter to Governor Sandoval.

This was our rally to "Restore Our Constitution" and our "State Sovereignty" by "We the People!!!"

Blessings

Early the next morning on Saturday, April 12th, I was busily working at my desk—the kitchen table—and had not noticed the family going into the master bedroom a few at a time. Carol came to the kitchen where I was reviewing the schedule for the day. She asked me if I had received a priesthood blessing yet. I answered that I had not, so she asked if I wanted one. Feeling very grateful for the opportunity, I responded quickly that I did.

Cliven and Duke, his son-in-law were in the bedroom and they invited me to sit on the wooden chair that had been placed in the center of the room. As they laid their hands upon my head, anointed me with sacred oil and gave me a beautiful blessing of peace and strength, I could feel the Holy Spirit descend upon my soul. The tears welled up in my eyes and my heart was filled with love and gratitude.

Following the blessing of comfort and direction I returned to the kitchen. It was 7:30 in the morning and everyone had departed to complete their individual assignments. The house was mostly empty and very quiet. I was watching the clock as I worked. When it said 9:00 a.m. I gathered up my camera, cell phone, and other things and headed for the front door. I noticed through the front window the body guards and militia men were still in the front yard. As I entered the living room, I was surprised to see Cliven all alone still sitting quietly on the couch. He was dressed and ready to go. I asked, "I thought the rally started at nine o'clock—aren't you supposed to be there?" He looked me in the eye and said, "I'm not leaving until I get word that the Sheriff has arrived." "Okay," I said, "I'll see you up there."

I jumped into my truck and left. As I approached the Check Point Area, I noticed the place was crowded with vehicles and people. I had a hard time trying to find a place to park. I got out of my truck and grabbed my "Title of Liberty" flag so that I could mount it on the new flag pole I had just purchased. I brought washers and screws but for some reason I had forgotten my screwdriver. Great! A lady passing by saw me with my arms full and offered to help me carry things and took the flag and pole. She said she had a zip tie and with the help of Kenna (Cliven's niece) they were able to attach it to the pole. Kenna was following behind me carrying the flag as we wound our way up the road and through the crowd. Just behind us was the Sheriff and his half dozen deputies. I turned around to see three or more trucks full of militia men all dressed up in their camo and gear. In the middle of them was a Hummer with a couple inside it, along with Cliven and Carol. I had never seen all these men before in their outfits and gear. I had overheard them earlier saying something about men being spotted on hill tops, but that was it. As the militia escorted Cliven and Carol through the crowd we stepped aside and let them through as they headed towards the stage—a flatbed trailer.

Volunteers pause for the National Anthem *(credit noisyroom.net)*

Cliven and volunteers heading for the wash *(credit nesaranews.com)*

Militiaman with American Flag at twilight

Title of Liberty Flag

Ryan Bundy began the program. After the prayer and Pledge of Allegiance we sang the Star Spangled Banner.

Then the most wonderful sight to see was the parade of 50 horses and riders as they marched across the bridge carrying the American Flag, the State Flag and Flags representing all the divisions of the US Military, Army, Navy, Marines, and so on. Solemnly they paraded past us and up the road in rank and order. As they reached the dirt road at the end of the cement barriers they single filed across the face of the hillside on the opposite side of the road. Kenna was holding the "Title of Liberty" flag and I told her to run over there and hand them the flag because it needed to be part of this. She pushed her way through the crowd with the flag high in her hands as she ran up the hill. Clancy saw her coming and reached out to receive the flag. He joined ranks with the others carrying flags.

The Title of Liberty Flag

The riders continued onto the second road as they began to spread out and faced the top of the hill at attention. They filled the second road and the riders carrying the flags climbed even higher towards the top. Then a lone horseman, (Arden Bundy, 15 years-old) rode his horse to the top of the hill and as he dismounted he dramatically planted the American Flag on top of the mountain as the crowd cheered them on. The yell came, "It's Bunker Hill!"

Arden planted the American Flag

Then one rider, leading a riderless horse representing the fallen soldiers who have died for this country, crossed the hill top behind the riders carrying the many flags. They came to rest on the top of the next hill in order and at attention. Clancy rode across the face of the hill with the "Title of Liberty" proudly waving in the air. The whole grand scene evoked a feeling of patriotism and the Spirit testified of the divinity of this Land. The song "This Land is Your Land" was racing through our minds!

<u>Cliven Bundy's Speech</u>

The Sheriff was offered the microphone. Very briefly he told us that he would be happy to sit down and negotiate some terms with the people. He didn't take long and then Cliven was welcomed to the microphone.

Cliven said to the Sheriff—

"Negotiations are past, we have been trying to negotiate for years even up 'til that last Tuesday when I was at your office. Today 'We the People' are going to tell you what ***our*** demands are! ... Sheriff, 'We the People' are asking this morning—disarm the Park Service at Lake Mead and Red Rock Park, claims you have jurisdiction over. Take your county bulldozers and loaders and tear down those entrance places where they ticket us and make us citizens pay their fees. You get the county equipment out there and tear those things down this morning! You disarm those Park Service people, you take a pickup, and I want those arms and 'We the People' want those arms picked up, don't we?"

Cliven with Sheriff Gillespie to his left
(credit forbes.com)

"Yeah", the crowd yells.

"Call the Virgin Valley Disposal and go up here to this compound and we want all of those arms from that compound today. We want those arms delivered right here under these flags in one hour! And media, are you here media? I want you to go to every place that they got a Federal Park Service Station and you watch those county machines tear down those places today in the next hour. If you do, report back to We the People in one hour. If they're not done then, we'll decide what we're going to do from this point on."

That's when Sheriff Gillespie and his deputies left and so did all the major media.

As Cliven began to speak about "We the People" and how we have to stand up for our Sovereignty, we suddenly noticed two

flocks of geese flying directly over the stage with a third even larger flock right behind them! A hush fell over the audience as Cliven and the people began to point at "God's Fly Over!" The whole time I had been at the ranch none of us had seen any geese and yet they came from the South towards the river. I kept watching them as they passed across the freeway, broke formation and began to swirl and hover right over the top of the cattle in the corrals. I shouted "They are circling the cattle!" I knew where they were because I had just flown over them myself!

I was taking video at the time and it brought back memories of Glenn Beck's "Restoring Honor Rally" in Washington DC in 2013 when we had a magnificent flock of geese fly over the reflective pond. All 1.5 million people in attendance shared a reverent and spiritual feeling that occurred at that time. Glenn Beck had not been totally on board in understanding where Cliven was coming from and I wanted to shout "Glenn, Wake Up! We have a triple fly over here today, the Lord is with us!" I have seen many mighty miracles at Glenn's events and I know that the Lord has blessed him and Glenn does listen to the Lord. That is not to say that there are no other men that are being inspired and blessed also. I compare it to a canoe being paddled down the river. We are all headed for the same destination. One person is pulling his oar on one side and one on the other side. Even though we don't both see it the same way and we have different approaches to our situations we have the same destination and hoping for the same outcome.

Ultimatum

We continued the program and Ryan sang all four verses of the Star Spangled Banner in his beautiful tenor voice. While waiting for the sheriff to return and report, people were spontaneously invited onto the stage to sing, speak, recite poetry and in general express themselves concerning the situation.

The hour went by and someone shouted, "It's been an hour and 10 minutes." Cliven really didn't want to hear that. He returned to the microphone. "Does anyone see the Sheriff or his deputies?" "No!" the crowd yelled. "Where is the Media that was supposed to return and report?" "Not here," some yelled.

Just then a metro police car drove by. Hoping it might be the Sheriff's report, Cliven asked, "should we give them any more time?" "Five minutes," was the answer.

All during this time I was texting on my cell phone to our Congressman from Utah, Chris Stewart, letting him know what was going on. He texted me back with "I just got off the phone with Neil Kornze, head of the BLM. They are backing down. They will be pulling out within the hour. You win! Don't do anything crazy! They are backing down."

April 9, 2014 Neil Kornze was made the head BLM Director by Senator Harry Reid.

A good question is, "How does a 35 year old man, with only two years in the Agency, get to be the Director?" asks Mark Reasbeck. Maybe it was because Neil, who is from Elko, Nevada, worked for Harry Reid as a senior public lands Advisor for eight years and in Jan. 2011 he joined the BLM. March of 2013 he was made the principle deputy director. He was endorsed by Sen. Harry Reid who said "Neil is just perfect for this position." He was challenged by Sen. John Barrasso, (R-Wyoming) who wanted to know how Neil Kornze's experience compared against several previous BLM directors who had 30 years of experience as land managers before receiving the director's job.

Obviously; it's not what you know, it's who you know!

Episode Four

Confrontation

Action

I hurried to the stage to show the text to Cliven but too late. He was already at the microphone.

"I guess he's not coming, his five minutes is up and the sheriff isn't here. Are we going to go and take our land back and declare Freedom and Liberty here in this land? Is God gonna be with us?" Cliven asked. "Yes!" the crowd yelled. "One thing I'm gonna do, Cliven Bundy is gonna turn cattle out on his farm. They're gonna go out on the open range where they belong. We're gonna go and take the rest of them out of the compound corrals up here above the freeway. This should be the Governor of Nevada's job, but he's actually inspected these cattle to go to California. So if they haven't gone to California yet, let's go get those cattle and all we gotta do is open the gates and let 'em back down on the river and they're home. OK, we need a little bit of safety here. We gotta go up the freeway, we're gonna block the freeway. When we get to the Toquop Bridge we're gonna get out of our cars and we're gonna go and open the panels. These horse people are gonna go up the power line road, gonna meet us at the Toquop Bridge. Common Cowboys, let's go Git'er Done!"

Everyone was racing to their vehicles. I wanted to follow Ryan to the wash to open the gates but by the time I got to my truck he was already five vehicles ahead of me. I couldn't get through and lost him. When I got to the freeway I began to weave in and out of the traffic and they moved over and let me through. At the end of the barrier I drove off the freeway where we could get others off safely. Someone had already cut the barb wire fence and I helped remove the metal posts so no one would puncture their tires. The people began to flood in by the hundreds and hundreds and the traffic on the freeway was backing up to a STOP! We even had others that had gone to the other side of the freeway to stop the traffic headed west.

In the confusion I parked my truck and raced down the hill to the wash, then realized that I had dropped my cell phone some place. I didn't want to back track so I began to spread the word to those around and those still coming down to let me know if someone comes across my phone. Now I had no communication with the outside world! I did have my camera along with hundreds of others.

(credit AP, dailymail.uk)

As I reached the bottom of the hill I was met by Ammon whose arms were outstretched. He instructed us not to enter the wash yet! There were agents parked in front of the fence panels that were crouched down behind their open doors in a defense pattern with weapons drawn. Being the curious person that I am I had to look through a mesquite bush there to observe for myself. Sure enough, there were the white Ranger trucks parked side to side with both doors open and men dressed in army looking gear. I pulled my head back behind the hill.

Ammon took charge and instructed us to wait until everyone had come down the hill to join us. There were more people still coming down. I would guess we had a couple of hundred when Ammon told us that we needed to have a prayer and asked who wanted to offer it. Before I realized it I blurted out, "Me"! My heart was very full and as we all knelt down in the sand I poured out my heart to the Lord for his guidance and protection. I expressed how much we love Him and this land He has given us. As I offered up the prayer we all felt the Spirit descend on us like a blanket of protection. Some say it was like we were suddenly in a bubble. Untouchable.

Wherefore, he will preserve the righteous by his power, even if it so be that the fullness of his wrath must come, and the righteous be preserved, even unto destruction of their enemies by fire. Wherefore, the righteous need not fear; for thus saith the prophet, they shall be saved, even if it so be as by fire. (1 Nephi 22:17)

<u>Advance</u>

We stood and together we formed a line a few deep and swung out and across the wash. The bull horns from the Rangers began to shout demands for us to "Stop and Disperse." We stood still as someone on our side instructed us to not do anything crazy. Don't try to be brave, just sit and wait for the horses. There were actually two overpasses above us and I asked if we couldn't move up together just a bit so we could wait in the shade. It was a very hot day and the shadow of the bridge was only 10 feet in front of us. In spite of all the shouts from the bull horns we slowly inched forward to the shade and stopped! The rangers/agents looked more like they were dressed for war. They never dropped their weapons they had pointing at us.

As I looked around at the people that were with us I noticed that there were "Oath Keepers," "militia men," body guards, family members, friends, patriots, men, women, and a couple of teens and some brave media. We could hardly tell what they were yelling in the bull horns because the sound would echo back under the two bridges. The little bit of wind was blowing towards the Rangers. I heard them say that those with rifles should leave the rifles back behind the bridges. There were only two men carrying rifles that I witnessed. There were mostly unarmed citizens! The men with rifles stayed back and put them down. We could also hear something about a Federal Court Order. Really? How does an unconstitutional illegal federal court order have anything to do with stealing private property? What a joke!

Volunteers wait under the bridge
(credit suindependent.com)

While some stood and some sat waiting in the shade a few thoughts raced through my mind. I knew in my heart that I was not going to die! I was forming a plan in case the men decided to open fire on us. Why did I wear a white hat and shirt of all days? The gentleman sitting in front of where I was standing kept inching up closer. I was trying to figure out how I could grab him if he got shot and roll with him behind a small, nearby mesquite bush, which really wasn't much protection. We waited, visited, and waited.

When Ammon noticed a couple of guys beginning to back off and retreat he called to all of us, "Don't back down, don't anyone back down. We must stand together for however long it takes. If it takes two days we will stay here. We will bring in food, water, toilets. Whatever it takes. Don't back down or we will lose the war!" Everybody stayed still.

Just like the prophet Elisha said, when being attacked by Syria: "And he answered, Fear not; for they that be with us are more than they that b*e* with them." (2 Kings 6:16)

We did have a young reporter from Alex Jones (www.InfoWars.com) that stepped out ahead and began to walk towards the armed rangers with his large camera in one hand and his other outstretched hand in the air to show he had no weapons. I was really waiting for them to shoot him but as he walked slowly towards them stopping now and again, he got closer and closer for the live video. I have to admit he was very brave or very crazy.

There were a couple of others that kind of got carried away and attempted to rush forward. We had to control these outbursts. I recall one man who was shouting and swearing up a storm. I walked up to him and patted him on the chest. "Please don't do that. Please don't be doing that; if we want the Lord to be with us we can't do that." I shook my head at him. He began to nod and said, "You're right, I shouldn't" and he quit! There were others that took the same stance to make sure we didn't let anyone get out of control.

More and more ranger vehicles were arriving with more men. They were stacking in rows just like in war. We could zoom in on them with our cameras. They looked like they were dressed in army fatigue only a different shade of green even to the helmets.

Horses and Riders

I learned later that as the horses and riders traveled across the desert, half way out were called to stop and kneel down in prayer. They did and were also given the same sense of assurance of safety and peace. They were led by Clancy Cox carrying the "Title of Liberty" flag. Clancy gave the riders instructions to stay in formation, don't break the lines, don't get brave or crazy—just be humble and stay together. No talking nor shouting. Just stay in formation.

Of course, the war over free agency has long been waged here on earth, and there are those today who are saying, "Look, don't get involved in the fight for freedom. Just live the gospel." That counsel is dangerous. Self-contradictory, unsound because part of the reason we may not have sufficient priesthood bearers to save the constitution, let alone to shake the powers of hell is because unlike Moroni, I fear, our souls do not joy in keeping our country free, and we are not firm in the faith of Christ, Nor have we sworn with an oath to defend our rights and the liberty of our country.

Moroni raised a "Title of Liberty" and wrote upon it these words: "In memory of our God, our religion, and freedom, and our peace, our wives, and our children." Why didn't he write upon it "Just live your religion; there's no need to concern yourselves about your freedom, your peace, your wives, or your children"?

The reason he didn't do this was because all these things were a *part of* his religion, as they should be a part of our religion today.

Should we counsel people, *"Just live your religion—there's no need to get involved in the fight for freedom?"* No, we should not, because our stand for freedom is a most basic part of our religion; this stand helped get us to this earth and our reaction to freedom in this life will have eternal consequences. Man has many duties, but he has no excuse that can compensate for his loss of liberty.

Horses

It was about an hour before the horses finally arrived. It was a sight for sore eyes! It was just like the Calvary had come. As they joined us under the bridge all the rest of us gathered together alongside, behind and among the horses, and began to advance toward the fence panels and agents. The shouts began to come across the bull horns for us to stop. We made it all the way to the second bridge. There were crowds of people up on top of the bridges who were shouting and cheering. We called to them to come down and join us. Some of them did. They began to climb over the concrete barriers and slide down the cement walls. One man on crutches even slid down. The traffic had been backed up but had finally opened up one very slow lane and as the vehicles would pass they would see what was going on and honk in support. It was truly amazing!

We continued forward very slowly. There was one older gentleman who had reached the fence and was yelling at the agents. I told Ammon to go get him. He approached the man gently and tried to persuade him to step back with the rest of us. The man was very upset and almost in tears as he half cried, "My son was just killed fighting for this Country and we cannot give up! We have to stop this Tyranny!" Ammon returned and left him at the fence. His heart was truly touched. The man was ready to die for the cause!

Latter-day Saints "devoutly believe that if the Constitution should be in danger of being over thrown, their lives, if need be, are to be offered in defense of its principles." (Harold B. Lee, *True Patriotism-An Expression of Faith,* April 13, 1941)

The next thing I knew Dave Bundy was on the other side of the panels and the cameras were rolling as Ammon talked with Daniel P. Love, Agent in Charge, and told him repeatedly; "*You* need to leave! We are not leaving! We are coming to release our cattle and you need to leave." Dan replies that he would allow only the Bundy brothers in to release the cows but Ammon stands firm and says again, "No. This is public land and *you* need to leave! All the cowboys will be coming in." Not long after this the County Deputies began to appear. Some of us were up to the fence panels by now and I was able to get some up close pictures of the rangers/agents.

Some of them did not look like Americans. They looked more like they were from the Middle East. One reporter told me that when he had approached them before today, when he called them by name (they had on name tags) they never responded to their own names. In fact they didn't even speak English, he said. I found that very easy to believe after seeing them myself.

The horses were carrying the American and Title of Liberty flags with them as we all waited under the bridge. Ammon, Dave, and Ryan Bundy were all there and Ammon told the Deputies that all we wanted to do was to open the gates and let the cattle out and we would do it however they wanted us to but our objective was to let the cattle out and we weren't backing down. Ammon cut a sign down off the fence that said: "CLOSED AREA Temporary Closure of Pubic Land in Effect 18 USC 1509. You may be officially charged with obstruction of a court order." Signs like it had been placed all over the roads every 30-50 ft. Ammon said he wanted it as a trophy!

We were instructed to back off the fence 10 feet, for whatever reason that was about but we obliged and retreated. Then we were told that we had to give them another 30 minutes to pack up their things and pull out. So we sat and waited another hour as all the men began to walk backwards still facing us. After a little ways they got in their vehicles and turned around and drove away slowly. We waited!

The deputies instructed us that we needed to all get back and line the wash as the cattle came out so nobody would get run over. He was only going to let the horses and the three Bundy sisters in to open the gates and let the cattle out. At first he told Ammon that they could only open one corral at a time and let the out but Ammon explained that would not be a good idea. We need to let them all go at once because they were going to travel quickly together to the water and these cowboys were very experienced and knew exactly how to work the cows. The deputy finally agreed.

Everyone was hugging and singing and breathing a sigh of relief. We could hardly believe it! We had won the battle, Not the War but at least the battle! I began to say, "This is just as important as the Boston Tea Party, The Battle of Bunker Hill, or Gettysburg" My thoughts went out to all those who were too

afraid to stand up. They missed it! They could have been a part of history and they missed it!

While we were waiting for the agents to pull out, the rest of us at the gate, mostly family, knelt down in a prayer of thanksgiving and gratitude! We knew it was only through the hand of the Lord that nobody was injured and we were able to accomplish this mission! God Bless America!!!

We were instructed by Ammon for everyone to back away from the wash so when the cattle came out we wouldn't spook them and cause a stampede sending them back to the compound. We all moved back down to the edges of the wash trying to be out of sight of the cattle, even though we wanted to take pictures of their release. We waited and whispered about the wonderful things that had just transpired. It wasn't long before a cowboy came from behind a cow. Shortly thereafter they all came. A man standing next to me was counting them. He said he thought he counted about 350 head. It was a beautiful sight as the cowboys followed up behind them all the way down to the river.

(credit Reuters, dailymail.uk)

(credit AP, dailymail.uk)

Hanging from the concrete barrier of the freeway hung a beautiful sign that read "THE WEST HAS NOW BEEN WON!"

(credit AP, dailymail.uk)

We all headed back to our vehicles and after I hiked up the hill I discovered that I had in fact dropped my phone inside my truck. Oh thank you, dear Father!

Not wanting to fight our way back to the freeway some of us drove the desert road. It was long and dusty and one motor home, not wanting to be left behind followed the crowd. He was doing pretty well until he hit a very steep downhill and steeper uphill. He finally lost his speed and got stuck. But to the rescue came a red 4-wheel drive Chevy and hooked a tow strap to the motor home and out they went!

That's the Cowboy Way—Leave No Man Behind!

Plan B

When we arrived back at Check Point we discovered that Cliven and Carol were waiting there along with some of the other people who were too afraid to go to the wash. By this time Cliven had decided that we were taking way too long and was ready to go take care of it himself. Cliven took Carol and a body guard and headed down to the river where he had his D-8 Cat. He had decided that he would drive that dozer up the wash and open the gate himself. They parked the Jeep and Cliven waded through the mud and brush to climb aboard his Dozer. He instructed his driver to follow him as he would take the dozer and push the mud, traveling back and forth to pack it down so the Jeep could drive across the river and not get stuck. As he climbed aboard the dozer he had a hard time getting it started. It was never like this, it has always been very dependable and it was troubling to him. What was going on? Finally he got it started and now it wouldn't go forward, only in reverse. He tried again and again but to no avail. Finally he stopped the dozer, got off and knelt down in the mud and brush to offer up a prayer. A very loud and strong message was sent to him. "This is not your job! Let those who are supposed to do it, do it". After a few minutes he got back to his feet and waded back to the Jeep. As he climbed in he shared the message with his wife and driver. He asked them to take him back to the Check Point Area to wait.

Cliven said that when he saw the people returning from the Standoff he witnessed a special light about them. They were confident and happy. They were all smiles and bubbling with excitement to rehearse the events that had just taken place. What joy and gratitude they felt to our Father in Heaven and the many angels that were with them!

We The People were back on the land and river that day.

Back at the compound, when the cowboys and women had arrived at the corrals, they discovered that there were a number of young calves that had been totally neglected. One cow had delivered a baby calf that fell outside of the pen and couldn't be reached by the mama. It was starving. Other little calves wouldn't be able to get to the water at all because the water troughs were way too tall for them to drink from. These cows had never eaten hay before and that's what they were now feeding them. Dave had help gathering all the weak cows and bulls and little calves into the horse trailer and brought them home where I helped Dave find and make milk and water bottles to try to get the calves to suck. Some of them were so weak they couldn't stand and we had to pour water down them and massage their throats to help them

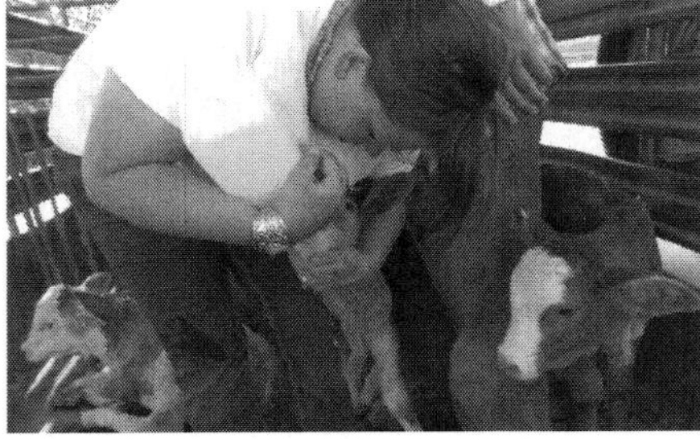

swallow. Along came Kenna and Stetsy to help. I knew the calves were in good hands.

There were speeches given at a rally afterwards on stage at Check Point Area where Stuart Rhodes, founder of Oath Keepers from Clark County, Nevada, said there were Representatives on their way here from 4 different States, but we had already taken care of the problem before they had arrived—but they were still coming. We can never thank these American's for all of their sacrifices they made to come and back us up and for the money they donated to help the family be able to give assistance to those in great need to get back home with fuel, food and such.

A number of men took a ride around the ranch and picked up some of the "Closed Area" signs for souvenirs after everything was over. We all returned and reported on the things that had taken place.

Cliven had instructed his children that morning that they should take the time and record the things that they experienced this day for their children and grandchildren. Briana's are recorded in the Closing Remarks at the end of this book.

That evening I jumped back into my truck and headed for home. I had to be to church the next morning at 9 am. I have a church calling I need to attend to.

"Next to being one in worshiping God, there is nothing in this world in which this Church should be more united than in upholding

and Defending the Constitution of the United States. If members of the Melchizedek Priesthood allow the U.S. Constitution to be destroyed, they not only forfeit their rights to the Priesthood, but to a place in the highest degree of glory as well." (David O. McKay, *The Instructor*, Feb. 1956, pg. 34)

That afternoon Senator Harry Reid said on Las Vegas Channel 13 news: "This is not over yet! Everyone at the Bundy Ranch is a domestic tourist. I mean domestic terrorist!"

That was an UN-nerving statement to some of the militia men and maybe a few citizens because being declared a domestic terrorist could mean that the Federal Government may arrest you anytime in anyplace and detain you for an indefinite amount of time with absolutely no charges. Thanks to the new NDAA law that was passed. Everyone was now in red alert status.

Ties That Bind

We began to research the ties. Thanks to the Drudge Report that went viral, according to the BLM's own public records, Harry Reid and his son Rory had a contract with ENN from Communist China to sell the Nevada State Land Bundy was on for a Solar Farm at a fraction of its value. Why?

(credit-conservativereport.org)

We had not yet heard the report by Infowars.com on the Drudge Report, which reported their findings from the BLM government website—

"In December, Clark County Commissioners voted unanimously to sell up to 9,000 acres of public land to the subsidiary at pennies on the dollar. The deal spurred local controversy. Separate appraisals valued the land at 29.6 million and 38.6 million dollars. The commission agreed to sell it to ENN for $4.5 million.

"The county did build in certain conditions before the project could begin, including milestones for jobs creation and investment." (It makes me wonder whose investment?) "ENN also must assure the county that it has a power company willing to commit to buying energy from the solar farm. But in the eight months since the commissioners approved the deal, no utility has signed a power purchase agreement."

As soon as it went viral, the BLM had that information removed from their website and also "Google" had its link removed, which had to be done according to their own rules by the owner of Google. How much influence does Harry Reid have?

Too Late! It was already posted across the nation thanks to Infowars.com. Tell me how any person has the right to sell State land to another country?

Does the Nevada State Constitution not exist? Does the State of Nevada not exist? It is being treated like a Territory, not a State. So where is the State Sovereignty?

I have come to discover that, despite some over-the-top conspiracy theories and occasional sketchy reporting, Alex Jones and the John Birch Society have been right all these years and the media and far left have done everything in their power to discredit them with false information.

EPISODE FIVE

Divine Intervention

It was Sunday morning on the 13th of April and Cliven was headed for church. He had a body guard on either side of him. They were a couple of rough looking men with tattoos. Cliven instructed them to leave their weapons in the vehicle. Trying not to be noticed, they walked in a couple of minutes late and went quietly into the overflow behind the sliding dividers. While they were still standing, right before they could be seated, a couple of elders pulled back the dividers and there they stood facing the stand! They were caught off guard. The looks on the Bishopric's faces were clearly those of surprise. Cliven said he'll never forget that moment. "It was kind of embarrassing."

Reconnaissance

That afternoon I had finished my business at home and was headed back to Bunkerville. Before I left my home I received a phone call from one of my children who had been informed that one of their friends had witnessed about 40 (they counted) white DNR (Department of Natural Resources) vehicles in town. That is very unusual for this area. Another person had overheard some of them talking at a local gas station about blocking off State Highway 89, 20, and a couple of others and that they were also blocking off Interstate 15 all the way to Las Vegas. They knew I was headed back and didn't want me to get picked up. Before I left town I had to drop my letters in the post office and bank and kept an eye out for any white DNR vehicles of which I had seen none. I called and left a message with my state representative asking what he knew about any meetings or convention of the DNR being in Kanab. I informed my family that I had a lot of work to do at the Ranch and I needed to get back. I promised I would be on the lookout and be very cautious.

While passing Colorado City, I received another phone call. This time from my sister in the Phoenix area. She was on the internet and found that the roads were closed down all the way to Las Vegas. She said that there were police cars, buses, paddy wagons that were there to arrest the people from the Bundy Ranch standoff. I told her I was on my way there and I would be on the lookout. Shortly another person texted me from Colorado informing me that all the hotels in Mesquite were filled with FBI and BLM agents to raid the Bundy Ranch. The word was that you couldn't find a room there because they were all booked up. I hit the freeway before St. George and filled up my truck with fuel in case I had to leave suddenly. I had to slow up because of the construction going on in the gorge.

I was very alert as I entered Mesquite. I drove through the parking lots of all the hotels and casinos. I knew I would be able to recognize the FBI and BLM vehicles if I saw them. I saw nothing out of order except there were quite a number of dune buggies and dirt bikes with an enclosed large trailer that was set up like a kitchen and another large trailer that was packed with things like camping supplies. I called and asked someone to check the internet to see if there was a race or rally of some sort scheduled for this area. The call came back negative.

My only thought was that perhaps the Agents were planning an attack at the ranch coming across the desert. I called the ranch house to see if everything was good. Everything seemed to be running the same as normal; everyone was safe. I then phoned to have another person call the hotels to see if they had any rooms available. They reported that there were plenty of rooms available. Feeling that it was all more false information being sent around the internet I reported back to those who had contacted me. But I did inform them that I appreciated their concern and to not send information when they receive it. I will be happy to debunk anything in question. It is always better to be safe than sorry!

As I drove past the Compound Wash there were still huge generators with giant lights on the empty compound. The Agents had not yet removed them nor the cell tower they had set up. The parking lot and camp were illuminated. I noticed that there were also four Bundy cows there that had obviously come back up the wash to the compound area looking for their calves.

It was very late by the time I arrived at the ranch and as I passed by the militia standing guard they waved me in. Everyone in the home was winding down for the night and I told them about the cattle. They would round them up in the morning but during the night they received a phone call that one of their cows had been killed on the freeway.

Inspiration

Monday April 14th at daylight the cowboys went and cleaned up the mess and drove the other cows home. Back at the compound Ammon said he felt that he was inspired for some unknown reason that he should dismantle every corral panel and lay them all down. He told the Sheriff's Deputies that he needed to lay down every panel. It made no sense but he promised to do it carefully and not hurt anything. They allowed him to do it, so he had a couple of the boys help him. While they were in the process, some of them noticed that the hired cowboys had dug a pit where they saw part of a cow's hide sticking out. They took pictures.

Harry Reid had announced that "This is Not Over Yet!" People across the nation heard his message and there was information that there was going to be a counter attack. One man ("Brooks" from Florida) told me that he got the information and immediately got his things in order in case he never returned, but he felt that he HAD to be there. This was so important to help the Last Rancher Standing! He traveled to Nevada and camped beneath the bridge until some of his Militia friends came and brought him up to the camp with them. He too, felt the Spirit of Peace and Love that was at the Ranch and from the Bundy Family.

When he returned home he did contact his local Sheriff and informed him of the truth about the Bundys.

His Father, who was opposed to his going along with his Uncle and Aunt, finally did his own homework and realized the importance of "Brooks" being there, and so supported him. He said that he believed that *everybody who had a soul should have been there!*

Debunking

My State Representative, Mike, called to let me know that there had been a convention in Kanab of the DNR for a couple of days and there were a lot of vehicles involved.

I called and asked my sister how she knew that the police and paddy wagons were really coming to the Ranch. She explained that they were on the freeway and in the video she could see the Bunkerville Exit sign. Then I asked her what time of day it was and she answered it was daylight. She sent me a link to the video. Wow, I had no idea. Not only were the police and paddy wagons at the exit but also there were two Apache helicopters supposedly ready to come in from the Mesquite airport. The video showed photos of a couple of armed Militia men who were set up behind the concrete Freeway barriers lying down with their weapons on the Agents below. I could hardly believe my eyes! What brave militia men to stand up to such tyranny. They were only there to protect the unarmed citizens. They later stated that the agents were stacking down below just like they do in the military in preparation for war! It was believed by all militia that the Agents intent was never to back down but to attack us! They said that they were strategically placed and had the Agents begun to shoot then that would be the militia's signal to return fire and they had the upper hand because of their location. The Agents had left themselves on the wide open lower ground.

It takes approximately 1 hour and 20 minutes to travel from Las Vegas to the Bunkerville exit. Calculating this from the time Sheriff Gillespie left the stage at the rally, he would have had to dispatch the police caravan immediately for them to arrive that close to the standoff, which would place them within three miles of reaching us and arresting everyone who was there.

The word from Neil Kornze Head of BLM that they were backing down was a lie! There was never any intention for them to back off. They were going to murder hundreds of innocent and unarmed US Citizens. It would have been a blood bath if the militia had not been there. Because of the prayers of the righteous, the Lord had stepped in and protected us! Thanks be to God for our Constitution, our Second Amendment, Militia Members, CSPOA (Constitutional Sheriffs and Peace Officers Association), Oath Keepers, and all the American Patriots! It is very scary to imagine what the outcome could have been. Another Waco?

I also received a phone call at the house warning us that the government was sending "halo" in. That is low flying planes with military men parachuting in and opening their chutes at a low altitude so as not to be seen. I went outside and checked the sky. It was dusk and I could see a couple of low flying smaller planes but I could not see anything coming from them.

A letter was sent out by Ryan W. Payne (Head of security at the Ranch house)—

On the night of Friday, April 25th 2014, on or about 18:30 PST, I became aware of a bit of intelligence related to the possibility of a drone strike on Bundy Ranch and any supporters in the Bunkerville area possibly approved by the United States Department of Justice. As there appears to be a massive misinformation campaign against our efforts to promulgate freedom in this area, unvetted information is difficult to react upon. However, one must error always on the side of caution; and as some authorities within the government that have control of assets that have been shown to be pitted against the people who actually possess the rights to their control have continued to espouse an official labeling of the people gathered at Bunkerville as Domestic terrorists, The People so labeled must surely be presumed to maintain a posture of readiness to respond should those entities espousing those ideas against The People utilize The People's assets against them and pursue further the aggressive actions taken against the employees of The People, the Bureau of Land Management as presented within the last couple of weeks.

For these reasons, when I became aware of the information regarding the potential for a drone strike, my first reaction was to seek clarification on the issue by vetting the source. That vetting process resulted in the request by Rep. Michelle Fiore, who was present on the conference call deliberating the issue, to put before the conference so gathered the necessity of non-necessity for a request of support in the defense of The People and the Bundy ranch from the Governor of the State of Nevada. (Governor Sandival) She was made aware that we assessed there to be a low probability of the follow through or factual nature of the information, but once again, when dealing with the protection of lives, liberties, and property, we must always take a position that errors on the side of caution in the interest of securing those treasures of a free people.

The unanimous agreement was reached that our advice was that she should make the request for support from the Governor in the up scaling of the defenses at Bunkerville and around Bundy Ranch in response to the possibility of a military strike that The People of this state have been presumed to be denied an effective means of defense against through the enforcement of the unconstitutional codes and regulations that have dissuaded The People from pursuing an effective means of maintaining within their direct grasp the necessary assets to affect that defense. But We The People are aware that we possess this Right from birth, as for the privilege and duty to pursue the maintenance of those rights and protect The People from incursions of them; thus it was a lawful request for the use of those assets that the Governor is presumed to maintain control over to protect The People from what has displayed itself as a threat of death from a foreign entity in regards to this land, which is his Governorship's duty to protect via his Oath of Office.

The Governor has as yet not responded in correspondence or action to my knowledge in anyway, non-action which can only be viewed as a dereliction in his duty to uphold his Oath of Office, and protect The People and their Constitution from all enemies foreign and domestic. For this reason I, Ryan W. Payne, craft this affidavit as my legal testimony as to my knowledge of the facts.

Eternally, Your most faithful and humble servant,

Ryan W. Payne

"We were told by the prophet Joseph Smith, that the United States Government and people would undermine one principle of the Constitution after another, until its whole fabric would be torn away, and that it would become the duty of the Latter-day Saints and those in sympathy with them to rescue it from destruction, and to maintain and sustain the principles of human freedom for which our fathers fought and bled. We look for these things to come in quick succession." (Statement of Erastus Snow, 1885. Journal of Discourses, vol. 26, pg. 226, May 31, 1885)

That night a blood moon was to appear. At about midnight, Cliven and I went out to watch it and take pictures. The nights

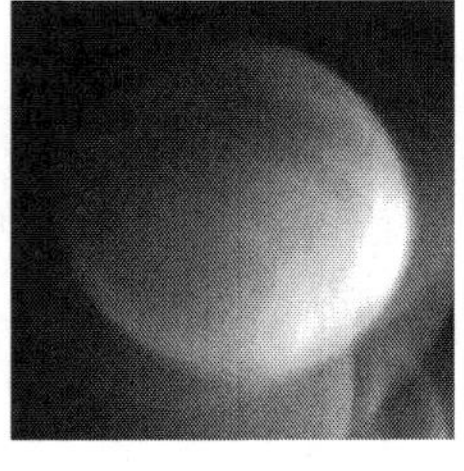

had been cool but this night it became very, very cold. Cliven went inside and brought Carol out along with a blanket. I was cold, but I didn't want to hold the blanket because I was having a hard time holding my camera perfectly still to get good pictures of the moon. It was exciting and interesting!

Criminal Acts

A group of family members had gone back to the Compound Area to search for any remaining evidence of their cattle. I sent my camera with them. They came across a large pit that had been dug by a backhoe and partly filled in with fresh loose dirt. They could see part of a cow hide sticking out of the dirt pile. They went back to the ranch and got their backhoe. As they began to dig they pulled from the pit four large bulls that had all been shot in the back of the head by a large caliber gun. Why? And the pit was large enough to bury many more cows.

(credit Tri-State Livestock News)

Up on top of the ranch they had already come across an area where there had been two bulls shot earlier, and one had been drug for over 1¼ miles behind a truck or some vehicle.

We were still missing a total of 39 cows according to the Agent's own records of the ones they had gathered, not including the two that never made it to the corrals.

On the morning news from Las Vegas, Harry Reid was holding a press conference honoring Sheriff Gillespie with the "Sheriff of the Year" award! Who is in bed with whom?

Episode Six

❧

Our Glorious Constitution

In one of the media interviews with Cliven's third son, Ammon Bundy, 38, the following was reported:

"Some have asked why my father didn't pay the grazing fee that the Federal Government demanded. This can be understood in two ways. One is founded on preemptive rights and the other upon State rights or State sovereignty. From our view, it is Constitutional rebellion.

"When my family rolled into this country in the 1800s, they began to tame the land and use if for survival, as others did in settling the rest of the United States. Each family claimed its stake and developed the area and understood that as long as the family was using the land or its resources, it was the family's to claim and share. When states were initiated into the Union, these rights or claims became more defined and further protected by state law as rights that could be sold, traded or even borrowed against.

"Now after over a hundred years of creating a preemptive right to the property through beneficial use of forage, water, access and range improvements, as recognized and protected by the state, the Federal Government claims that the land is not state land but U.S. Territory and theirs for the taking or charging of fees.

"So here we stand with some questions: Is this land Nevada state land or U.S. Territory? If state land, then my father's rights are

recognized and the Federal Government has NO claim to charge for something that is not it's to claim.

"If it is U.S. Territory, then Nevada is not a sovereign state. Less than 20% of Nevada is declared by the Federal Government to be private or state property. The rest the Federal Government claims as its land to do with as it pleases, and the people of Nevada have no rights to it.

"Now some more questions: Should the people of Nevada have the right to govern their own state? Why did the Federal Government retain almost 90% of Nevada land after statehood? Does the U.S. Constitution give the Federal Government the right to retain state lands?

"A good study of these questions will answer why Cliven Bundy refuses to pay an entity for something that is not theirs.

Again quoting (underlining is by the author for emphasis):

The U.S. Constitution Article 1: Section 8 spells out exactly the powers of Congress, including—

To exercise exclusive Legislation in all Cases whatsoever, over such District (not exceeding ten Miles square) as may, by Cession [permission] *of particular States, and the Acceptance of Congress, become the Seat of the Government of the United States, and to exercise like Authority over all Places* purchased *by the Consent of the Legislature of the State in which the Same shall be, for the Erection of Forts, Magazines, Arsenals, dock-Yards, and other needful Buildings;—And*

To make all Laws which shall be necessary and proper for carrying into Execution the foregoing Powers, and all other Powers vested by this Constitution *in the Government of the United States, or in any Department or Officer thereof.*

Article [X] states—

The powers not delegated to the United States by the Constitution, nor prohibited by it to the States, are reserved to the States respectively, or to the people.

And nothing more!!!

Again I repeat: Were any of the lands in the 13 Western States that the Federal Government lays claim to ever purchased? Did those states sell their lands to the Feds? Are these lands not more than 10 miles square in size? What about the National Parks? Did the States sell them these properties also? The answer is NO!!! Therefore the Federal Government has no authority or rights to govern nor police these states. These lands are the States' respectively and the States have jurisdiction over them the same as all the other States that were admitted into the Union! If these states had control of their own lands, then they would be able to prosper and would even have enough resources to pay off the national debt!

For there are many yet on the earth among all sects, parties, and denominations, who are blinded by the subtle craftiness of men, whereby they lie in wait to deceive, and who are only kept from the truth because they know not where to find it. Therefore, that we should waste and wear out our lives in bringing to light all the hidden things of darkness, wherein we know them; and they are truly manifest from heaven – These should then be attended to with great earnestness. Let no man count them as small things; for there is much which lieth in futurity, pertaining to the saints, which depends upon these things. You know, brethren, that a very large ship is benefited very much by a very small helm in the time of a storm, by being kept work ways with the wind and the waves. Therefore, dearly beloved brethren let us cheerfully do all things that lie in our power; and then may we stand still, with the utmost assurance, to see the salvation of God, and for his arm to be revealed. (D&C 123:12-17)

In an interview with Oath Keeper Founder, Stuart Rhodes, Jerry Delamose from New Hampshire representing his 9/12 group stated—

"We were called by God to come. We traveled over 2,700 hundred miles in 41 hours. We are a politically active group. I am a Marine

Veteran. We are fighting a lawless government. We created our 9/12 group because Glenn Beck preaches Liberty and I wish he was here to see this. We all pray together. (Emotionally) I am with the Best American's There Are!! 'Semper Fidelis'—always faithful.

"Dave Berry, Ex-Marine from Las Vegas, attended the first Oath Keeper convention in Las Vegas in 2009. I believe he was inspired to do so just as many others of us that were there! I was invited to attend by Sheriff Richard Mack and I was very surprised at how many were inspired to come and stand together. We were all inspired to do the same actions in each of our different parts of the country, and yet we never knew each other before. Dave also came to Bunkerville as an Oath Keeper. There was a call to all Oath Keepers in the country to come and stand watch. Their motto is 'Not On Our Watch!'"

Mission Statement by Operation Mutual Aid

Militiamen, Freedom Fighters, Soldiers, Patriots All

Who?

A coalition of States Militias, Patriotic Civilians, Individual Freedom Fighters, and Media Relations personnel from Patriotic political activism groups, in conjunction with local Law Enforcement if and where applicable.

What?

Defense of public and private property, lives, and liberty to exercise God-given rights, seen plainly in the laws of Nature, and codified in the Declaration of Independence and Bill of Rights, at the request of such parties in need of such defense, and the documentation and archiving of all defensive actions taken by the coalition for accurate and prompt reporting to all concerned public venues and media.

Where?

Defensive posture shall be taken up in the optimum tactical position in relation to the people or property in need of such defense. All local laws not in violation of the U.S. and subject States Constitution shall be observed. All laws in violation to the U.S. And subject States Constitution are hereby considered null and void, the enforcement of which most likely represents the need for such defense as herein outlined.

When?

As the nature of a Quick Reaction Force is understood, a defensive posture will be taken up in the shortest amount of time possible for the allocation of the necessary defensive resources to the location determined. Minimum force size will be determined by the leadership of the coalition.

Why?

As had been the case throughout recorded history, and reasonably assumed throughout unrecorded history, governments instituted amongst men for the protection of private lives and of their institution, and, specific to these United States, such governments have done so in complete and utter violation of the documents which established them by the free will of the people who established it in pursuit of its own goals.

At such a point as the government intends to use the physical power granted it by those who implemented it against them, it then becomes the responsibility of the people themselves to defend their country from its government, and to generally revert to the process outlined by the Declaration of Independence to absolve such government of its power, or separate from it to be freed from its oppression. As this coalition is intended for the defense of the populace from enemies foreign and domestic, the latter path shall be left to the determination of that populace, and we shall guarantee them the freedom to make that choice in accordance with man's God-given Liberty, the ideas espoused in the Declaration of independence, the Constitutions of the several States, the Constitution of their union, and the Bill of Rights, so help us God.

Operation Mutual Aid, Oath Keepers, CSPOA
(Constitutional Sheriffs and Peace Officers Association).

There was also representation from Sea to shining Sea to protect the Bundy Family and Friends and to stand up for "We The People."

"RESISTANCE—because if we fight we might lose, but if we don't fight we've already lost!"

(Quote by some of the Militiamen)

"THIS IS THE LAND OF THE FREE BECAUSE OF THE BRAVE!"

"IF NOT ME, THEN WHO? IF NOT NOW, THEN WHEN?"

So you see, it just takes one to stand up and others will follow in righteousness.

A Moral & Righteous People

Cliven had been trying to attend the St. George Temple and I had to clear his schedule so he could attend this morning asking for help from the Lord. He was praying every day for inspiration.

He didn't want to do anything unless the Lord had inspired him to do it.

***Fifth:* The Constitution was designed to work with only a moral and righteous people.**

"Our constitution," said John Adams (first Vice-President and second President of the United States), "was made only for a moral and religious people. It is wholly inadequate to the government of any other."

In recognizing God as the source of their rights, the Founding Fathers declared Him to be the ultimate authority for their basis of law. The Constitution was conceived to be such an expression of higher law.

And when their work was done, Madison wrote: "It is impossible for the man of pious reflection not to perceive in it a finger of that Almighty hand which has been so frequently and signally extended to our relief in the critical stage of the revolution." (*The Federalist,* no.37.)

As people called, the message for me to deliver to them was that there are 3,100 counties in this country. All the people should contact their local sheriff and find out if he is truly a Constitutional sheriff or not. They are to demand that he disarm every Federal Agent in their county because none of those agencies have policing authority, only sheriffs have that power.

If the Sheriff won't do that, then you will know he isn't upholding the Constitution and this is the year to vote them out of office and replace them with someone who will. This is very important! I also asked each one of them to continue to pray for all of us and our country.

"We the People" have allowed the government to ignore one of the most fundamental stipulations of the Constitution—namely, the separation of powers.

Cliven had responded to so many interviews his voice was giving out. He had told his story over and over and until he thought everyone should already know everything about it. The problem is each reporter is different, every media source has their own followers. That means he had to keep telling the story.

I didn't want to restrict any of the media from getting their story. There were so many of them and I scheduled him tight.

We had people call with all sorts of helpful information. Each was trying to help us get out of this situation using all sorts of legal means. We had whistle blowers and secret documents. I felt like I was a secret agent on a mission to gather proof! At one time I was really catching on to some great information and talking it over with Carol, Cliven's wife. We both felt like it made a lot of sense. We tried to talk with Cliven about it and when I started getting people to support the idea, Cliven called us into "The Bedroom" for a conference. He asked me to explain just exactly what I thought we should do. He let me explain it outright and then looked me squarely in the eye and said, *"The Lord didn't tell me that; I'm waiting for further instructions!"*

It was like a rude awakening! How could I possibly argue with that? In other words, the Lord was saying, "You're not in charge Shawna, I am!" I had experienced that before so I knew Cliven was speaking the truth!

We had people call and offer to pay the $1 million to just end this thing and be free and clear from everything. I thanked them for their generosity and explained that this fight was far more than that. We are not trying to get out of the fight but to "Restore the Constitution" and fight for "State Sovereignty."

We must bring to light that we do have a tyrannical government and expose them for what they really are. Remember the words of Thomas Jefferson—"The Greatest Danger to American Freedom is a Government that ignores the

Constitution." Also—"The People May Abolish A Government Which Has Become Tyrannical."

The question still remains, "How do we do that?"

What many fail to realize is that most of these federal agencies are unconstitutional. They concentrate the functions of the legislative, executive, and judicial branches under one head. In other words, they have power to make rulings, enforce rulings, and adjudicate penalties when rulings are violated. They are unconstitutional because they represent an assumption of power not delegated to the executive branch by the people and the people have no power to recall administrative agency personnel by their vote.

Cliven is trying to show us the way which is to peacefully stand up and say NO MORE and it takes all the people standing up together. The more people, the stronger the message!

Cliven has been willing to put his life, his livelihood, his ranch, even his family's lives, his fortune and his sacred honor on the line for this! Yes, it was said by many afterwards: Cliven is the New American Hero!

People kept calling in with support and encouraging words. The media came and wanted more and more photos of Cliven, the family and the Ranch. Now we were not only doing interviews but photo ops.

EPISODE SEVEN

Calm Before the Storm

The Picnic

Here it was Wednesday, April 16th, and we were still answering phone calls and gathering information. Cliven came up with this great idea that we should have a picnic and invite all of our patriots to come for a huge cookout and entertainment on Friday night. Because I had planned and executed many large gatherings before, I almost lost my breath. How in the world are we going to pull that off in so short a time? We have to notify everyone and gather all kinds of food because he wanted to feed them all for free and let them swim or wade in the river because this is their public land. He wanted them to feel the sense of Freedom again!

We all began racing in all directions. Bailey and Brianna got on the internet and began looking for entertainment. I called my friends who sing Western songs and do cowboy poetry. We all started inviting everyone we could reach. Carol and girls started hitting Costco stores to buy up all the hamburger and hotdog buns, napkins, water, condiments and hot dogs. Ammon packed up all the food he could find with tables and grills as many things as he could carry and headed for the ranch. It was wild! Everyone had a job and still had to do ranch chores on top of that plus still feed militia and body guards.

About 10 p.m. Brianna called and said she had scheduled Ron Keel, "The Metal Cowboy," who had offered to come at his own expense. (We had a very limited budget)! We pulled him up on the computer and listened to some of his music. It was kind of like rock-n-roll country music. I was thinking that Cliven might not agree with that but Brianna was determined!

At 11:30 p.m. Bailey came in and said she had just received a confirmation that a hot new patriotic rock-n-roll band from New York, Madison Rising, just responded. Their booking agent just picked up on our request and even though it was Easter Weekend they really wanted to do this. Bailey asked them how much it would cost and she was informed that it would cost them $5,000 just to book their flights and get their equipment here. Wow! We don't have that kind of money but the agent assured Bailey that they would raise the money starting that moment.

Within an hour they called back (remember it is about 2:30 a.m. Eastern Time now) and they said they had raised $1,800. By the time we went to bed they let us know that they had raised all the money and were packing their equipment and on their way. This is now early Thursday morning. We also listened to a couple of their songs on the internet and they too were a little Rock-n-Roll. The agent told Bailey that the band had lots of followers and would probably help with a good turnout. "How many people do you think?" asked Bailey. "Not more than 10,000," she replied.

Bailey panicked. When she told Carol and me, we almost choked. How are we going to feed 10,000? I figured it was Easter Weekend and perhaps most people already had family plans. Vegas was close and still could give us a big turn out if they were informed. It was hard to sleep at all.

The next morning was a rat race. We were calling everyone to help and bring in as many barbeque grills that anyone in driving distance could carry. Cliven had already had two cows killed and cooling for hamburgers. He called and had two more butchered just in case. We didn't want to run out. We made another trip to the Costco stores in Las Vegas to gather more buns and hot dogs. All day was racing to and fro.

The next morning we were still getting port-a-potties set up for all these people and trash cans, parking areas and everything. The kids were so responsible and stepped up beautifully. I was totally impressed with how it came together. By about 1 p.m. Ron Keel and his wife arrived at the Ranch House. It was a real pleasure to meet them. Such nice, kind and wonderful people they were. Never complained and offered to help as we were trying to get the stage and sound systems with generators set up for the entertainment. Dave was down flipping hamburgers all night and people came bringing salads, cakes and other goodies to eat. We had volunteers to help with the chairs and tables set up. People volunteered to help with the food.

We had T-Shirts that had been donated for sale and volunteers to help sell them. It was awesome.

T-shirts had been donated from Arizona, Nevada, and California. Such generosity of truly American patriots! The airplane was a little late getting to Vegas and then there was an accident closing down the freeway for a little while delaying the Madison Rising Band. We began anyway and had some wonderful Western Music by Kenny Hall. We had some great Cowboy poetry by Paul Bliss. The families were playing in the river with their children and all of them received a donated "hot wheels car." We visited and laughed and ate. Everyone was having a great time. As it began to get dusk, the "Metal Cowboy" Ron Keel took the stage and put on a great show.

Paul Bliss, poet

By this time, Madison Rising had arrived. He began to perform at about 10:30 p.m. They were fantastic! Cliven got up, said a few words and thanked everyone for coming and helping and hoped everyone was having a good time. The cheers went up. We didn't have 10,000 people by the way but we did have 1,500 to 2,000 I would guess. It was a wonderful night indeed. A few people drove back home that night and others decided to camp out there on the river. A George Washington (look alike)

came on Stage and quoting George Washington said, "Not Words But Deeds." Then we joined with him as he knelt in prayer using the words of George Washington's prayer at Valley Forge.

The crowd was very touched and our patriotism was very high that night! People gathered around trying to get pictures with Cliven and George Washington. I knew "George" for a number of years now as we had attended a number of different presentations and programs at the same time and had mutual friends. As he and his friends were milling around through the crowd he told me that they had to leave to go back home in the morning but they really wanted to interview Cliven to add to the ending of their new movie "Ride a Pale Horse—Part II" and also re-enact the horses as they left the Toquop Wash on Saturday. Well, I said, you just happen to be talking to the right person. I do Cliven's scheduling. I let them know that Cliven was scheduled to leave home in the morning by 8:00 a.m. to bless one of his new grand babies. But, I said, "How early do you get up?" Cliven is up very early and if you could be here by six o'clock a.m. I could get you in. He might be upset with me, but he'll do it!" They were very excited and promised to come even earlier to be all set up and ready for him.

There were lots of folks who tried to help clean up most of the things before they left and the rest was left for the morning. At the house we were busy trying to find places to put the things away.

Documentary Filming

Before we went to bed I told Cliven that he had an appointment for this documentary movie in the morning at 6:00 o'clock. He looked at me, gave me the eye and then a heavy sigh, and I knew we were in! I assured him it was very good publicity and it would help further the cause when people saw this movie!

Early the next morning the video crew arrived as promised. I got Cliven ready to talk with them and tried to run interference to keep the setting free of militia and everyone else as they needed silence on the set. I also asked Clancy and Arden to get the cowboys (of those who were still at the Ranch) rounded up so that we could go to the river and re-enact our winding up scene releasing the cattle. It took half the day, but we got it done.

It was Easter weekend and there had been a phone call from some thoughtful people who were sending Easter Baskets to all the little grandchildren at the ranch. It was time for me to get back home to spend Easter with my family.

While Cliven and Carol were at church there came a young reporter from Canada that really wanted to interview Cliven. This was out of the norm. We always observe the Sabbath Day to keep it holy and attend our meetings. Cliven made an exception for this young lady. She was from a long distance and only had this day to visit so he relented. Just outside the chapel he met up with her. She was so impressed and really did a good interview with him.

"Even this nation will be on the very verge of crumbling to pieces and tumbling to the ground, and when the Constitution is upon the brink of ruin, this people will be the staff upon which the nation shall lean, and they shall bear the Constitution away from the very verge of destruction." (Joseph Smith prophecy, July 19, 1840, Church Historian's Office, Salt Lake City)

We must be righteous and moral. We will not seek to receive what we have not earned by our own labor since the government owes us nothing. We will keep the Constitutional laws of the land and look to God as our Lawgiver and Source of Liberty.

I arrived that evening and I spoke with Cliven before going to sleep. He was concerned as to why there had been no Latinos or Blacks at our picnic on Friday night. None of us remembered seeing any of them there.

Subterfuge

Monday morning to my surprise there arrived at the front door two well-dressed Mexicans and their camera man. I usually do all the scheduling and I didn't know anything about this interview. Someone must have scheduled them either Saturday afternoon or Sunday while I was away. The phone is usually turned off on Sunday because we need the break and to keep the Sabbath Day holy. Besides that, we would receive calls all hours of the night because of time differences across the world.

The men came in and acted very excited to talk with Cliven. I sat in the living room with them during the interview. Cliven told them how much he appreciated the Latino because of their love of their families and what hard workers they were. He told a story about a time he remembered when they would come and work in the fields, there was a pregnant woman who was in the field picking radishes. When she had a fist full of radishes she left the field, walked into the weeds, delivered her baby, wrapped it in one of her skirts, left it in the bushes and returned to work, still holding that fist full of radishes! He has never forgotten it.

Then on the other hand he said that the Blacks have been so oppressed by the government that the fathers can't even live with the families because they get a welfare check. Now there are many, many young people who have no influence from their fathers. Of every ten black men, nine will be jailed because they simply have nothing to do. The women are aborting their babies by the thousands. Even though slavery was a terrible thing, he said, it would almost be better for them to still be slaves and picking cotton. At least they would have something to do.

Cliven told the men that we are celebrating freedom from this Tyrannical Government and he wanted them to come. He said we were going to have another picnic this Friday and we want it to be especially for our Latino and Black friends.

These men acted really excited. They spoke some English but mostly Spanish. Sometimes they spoke so fast I couldn't understand everything they said, but they did say that they had a website and that they would provide the entertainment and invite everyone. We would provide the food for them. They were happy as they left the Ranch and we were excited for them to come.

It was that afternoon that we received word that Cliven's cousin, Owen's wife Anna Lou Bundy, had passed away in St. George. Her funeral would be in St. George on Wednesday. She happened to be one of my mother's closest friends growing up there and I planned to attend to represent my family.

Evidence Gathering

That afternoon we sent a few people to go dumpster diving. It was a very stinky mess but they brought back boxes full of information. We sifted and sorted and tried to save anything of any value. We uncovered maps, names, dates, places, payroll, hotel bills, empty bullet boxes and all such things. It was a pot of gold at the end of the rainbow! It took hours but it paid off.

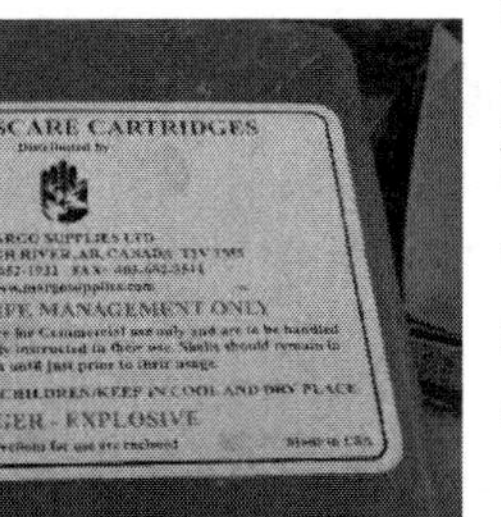

Tuesday we waited but heard nothing from the Mexican men. We began to wonder and asked one of the boys to check on them. There was no response all day. I spent most of the day on the phone and scheduling media besides helping to sort out the information. I went home late that evening so I could get my clothes to attend the funeral the next morning.

On my way to St. George I received a call from one person and then another asking if Cliven was a racist. "What! Of course not!" I said. They proceeded to tell me that the media had now been declaring him a racist and were disassociating themselves from him as fast as possible. It was going viral across the nation! People would call and tell me to tell him to "Keep his mouth shut! Every time he speaks he is digging a deeper hole!" My mind was racing as to what had happened. I was sure that the media had spun it but who and when? I asked what was said and as they repeated things I began to remember from the interview with the Latinos. They surely wouldn't have done that would they?

Carol called asking which chapel the funeral was at. Ryan was apparently there in St. George looking for it. I called Ryan and tried to give him directions. I told him I would pick him up if he wasn't there by the time I arrived.

Another call came and I was informed that Glenn Beck was denouncing Cliven and declaring him a racist. Cliven may not be politically correct, he may not be the best public speaker, and he may not be the best speller or the most educated. But one thing is for sure, He Is No Racist! He loves all people and has a heart of gold. He is a man of God and a wonderful patriarch and family man. Nobody I know is perfect! I was scrambling trying to find a contact we had for Glenn. Glenn of all people should understand the media spin!

I saw Ryan at the stop light just as I pulled into the chapel. I waved him down and we slid quietly into our seats as the funeral had already begun. It was a beautiful service and we visited for only a second as they were headed to the cemetery. Ryan had no vehicle, so I offered him a ride to the cemetery. Just as we got there he got on the phone with a Glenn Beck representative. I stood watching the burial as Ryan stood under a tree still on the phone the whole time. He arrived to give a few hugs and I told him I needed to get back to the Ranch. I dropped him off at the church and headed out.

Press Conference

Just as I hit the freeway I realized that we needed Ryan to speak at the press conference at 1:00 p.m. I whipped back around and headed for the chapel. I called Ryan on his cell phone and told him he was the one that needed to speak to the press. I asked him to come outside of the church because I was on my way back to pick him up. When I arrived he was standing on the sidewalk. We raced back to his job site to get a couple of his things from his work truck. Time was slipping by quickly. Back on the freeway we headed towards the gorge. I asked Ryan to call the ranch and tell them that we were on our way and to stall the press conference. We lost cell service and I asked Ryan to bounce off me the things he was going to say. He would think and then we would discuss. All of a sudden I remembered "Jason Bullock," a young black marine who was a body guard at the house. He was a good, kind and wonderful young man. He'd been there for days and knew Cliven well by now. He would be a great advocate for the truth. We sped past Mesquite and on to the exit. I told Ryan I would slow down and drop him off at the Check Point Area. He would have to race down to the stage. It was already 12 minutes past 1:00. I would hurry to the Ranch and grab Jason and bring him back here. Ryan jumped out of the truck as I slowed down and headed for the stage. As I drove across the bridge I could see Cliven was already on the stage. I called Ryan's cell phone. "Hurry," I said, "he's already on stage. I'll be right back." When I arrived at the house there was no Jason. Cliven had already thought of that and had taken him to the press conference. Whew! I called Ryan again and told him Jason was already there. Ryan informed me that his Father was doing a great job and he couldn't have done better himself.

Jason did get up and speak. He told the media that Cliven was not a racist and that he was a wonderful loving man. He even went so far as to say, "I love that man, he is like my grandfather and I would take a bullet for him if needed!"

Media Spin

The phones had gone crazy again and when Carol would receive a nasty call from someone who didn't really want to talk but just scream and be very foul and nasty, she would tell them, "Thanks for calling—I get a dollar for every phone call" and would hang up. It was great! I, on the other hand, was able to talk to most of the people and try to educate them as to the media spin. There were so many who would always say the same thing about wanting me to tell him to keep his mouth shut and let him have a spokesman for him. I figured that must be what the media or internet has been suggesting as the answer. The most interesting thing was that there was not one single phone call from a black person who was upset! One black person called and stated that what Cliven said was true and that he (Pastor Manning from Harlem, New York) had been preaching that to his congregation for years, including that he used to be a slave who picked cotton. Now I knew it was a plan to get Cliven out of the media because he was gaining too much positive attention and becoming the "New American Hero!" They had to do something because the American People were beginning to stand up!

I discovered that it was CNN who had spun it. Monday after Cliven's interview with the Latino's he was still in the same mind set when he went to the press conference. He had recited some of the same speech he had given to the Latino's that morning. I should have known because CNN has been funded and influenced by those wealthy people who are trying to control our world. They use the media to slant everyone into the way they want the peoples' mind set. In other words lies, lies, and more lies.

It didn't surprise me that they didn't air Jason's whole speech! The media pulled the "Race Card" and they began to drop us like a hot potato! That was the plan and the major media went with it! I have to say that we are ever so grateful for the new age media, such as: YouTube, Facebook, Blogging, Tweeting, Truth Tellers, and other media that have thousands of followers on the internet. Guerrilla Media with Pete Santilli, InfoWars with Alex Jones, WND from Canada and many other worldwide media that stayed with the real story. In fact there are fifty-two nations who have been following this "Stand Against Tyrannical Government." They are following our every move and hoping and praying so that they too might be able to save their own countries and people.

Here it is Wednesday evening and still no word from the Latinos. The next morning Kenna was assigned to follow up on them so we knew how many to prepare for. How much hamburger did we need? Cliven had already had two more cows killed and ground into hamburger. She finally got one of them on the phone but she couldn't understand what they were saying. She went up to the Check Point Area and got a family friend who was also a Mexican and asked him to come down and talk to these guys. When he hung up the phone with them he said, "Pull up their website. I have a feeling they're not as popular as they said. They were talking so fast and most of it wasn't making any sense." We pulled up their site only to discover that they only had 19 followers and one comment. Oh no, who was going to be coming to the picnic? What were we going to do for entertainment?

We began to call everyone we could to have them invite all of their friends. It was like a black cloud had come over us and the depression was palpable. Everyone was moping around shaking their heads. We still had militia there, thank goodness, and we still felt safe but things seemed very dark and dreary. I spent time sorting through the phone messages trying to get them filed in some kind of order so that we could reply to them. We were making thank you lists and legal information lists, and such things. People still coming to feed the calves and bringing food.

It was very hard to sleep that night.

Disconcerting Discoveries

While searching for more dead cattle on top of the butte some of the men found someone had unearthed a grave of one of the two old prospectors buried there. In this small fenced grave yard were laid to rest Arthur S. Coleman 1879-1958 and William H. Garrett 1880-1961. We called the sheriff's office, who sent out two officers to investigate.

The grave of Arthur S. Coleman had been dug up and the body exhumed. Who would do such a thing? We took pictures along with the deputies and discovered a sales receipt in the weeds from a store in Mesquite that read Mesquite Food L (something) that was dated 4/10/14. Guess who was in control of the land at that time? Nobody was allowed to drive up there because of their "Closed Areas!"

What kind of people are we dealing with?

The next day we received a call from an official from Overton Beach who said they found an injured calf and wanted us to come

and pick it up. Clancy went and got the little calf. It was pretty beat up and dehydrated. He had cuts on his nose and his poor tongue was almost cut in two. He also had a weak back leg so he could hardly stand up. It was very sad to see. Clancy brought it into the front yard and laid it gently beneath the tree in the shade. Michele Fiore was there and so were many others. Clancy tried to get it to drink water and nursed it all day. Cliven came and checked it over. All day long they worked with it.

As I lay on the couch that night about midnight, Kenna couldn't sleep because she felt so sorry for this poor little calf. She didn't want it to be alone. She felt it was calling to her and she got off her bed, took her blanket and pillow and went out and lay next to it until 3 am when the little calf finally passed away.

I awoke about 5 o'clock a.m. and knelt by the side of the couch to pray in the silent darkness of the roof.

CNN Interviews

At 6:00 a.m. on April 24th, Cliven had an interview with CNN down at the river. Clancy, Stetsy, Cliven and I drove down to the river with the little dead calf wrapped in a blanket and a box full of nursing bottles. Cliven was carrying the calf. He stood looking out over the river as the sunlight was just beginning to break across the horizon, the hurt and pain evident in his heart. The media can be cold and cruel.

They put up a table and had Cliven lay the calf down on top of the blanket along with the box of bottles. They had no intention of showing that on their news station. They only took pictures of Cliven's head and shoulders. The anchor man who was interviewing him from New York (I think) said, "Nobody wants to see a dead cow!" Cliven's response was, "The American people don't want to see a dead cow but would they rather see dead people?"

The media were trying to get Cliven to apologize for saying something about the Blacks. Cliven still didn't see what he said about the Blacks was wrong, but he reached down and took off his boot and, after shaking the sand out of the hole in the side of his boot, said, "I better remove my boot before I stick my foot in my mouth again." That was his way of saying that when you say something wrong you put your foot in your mouth, and when you do, it is pretty hard to swallow, especially if you have a boot on your foot. I don't think the media caught that.

Jason Bullock was also interviewed by CNN. He must not have said the things they wanted to hear because they cut his interview off quick!

Cliven looked with sadness out over the Virgin River holding the little calf that had died just a couple of hours ago. His cattle dying, his children being attacked, the media calling him a racist—what a heavy heart he must have had! The sunlight was just peaking over the horizon.

After we left, I rode with Clancy and Stetsy to bury the calf. It was a very solemn moment. It represented yet another tragedy on the ranch.

On April 25, Cliven sent out a press release—

We are Trading One Form of Slavery for Another

What I am saying is that all we Americans are trading one form of slavery for another. All of us are in some measure slaves of the Federal Government. Through their oppressive tactics, they tell the ranchers how many cows they can have on their land, making that number too low to support a ranch. The BLM has driven every rancher in Clark County off the land, except me. The IRS keeps the people of America in fear, and makes us all work about a third or a half of the year before we have earned enough to pay their taxes. This is nothing but slavery from January through May. The NSA spies on us and collects our private phone calls and emails. The government dole which many people in America are on, and have been for much of their lives, is dehumanizing and degrading. It takes away incentive to work and self-respect. Eventually a person on the dole becomes a ward of the government because his only source of income is a dole from the government. Once the government has you in that position, you are its slave.

I am trying to keep Martin Luther King Jr.'s dream alive. He was praying for the day when he and his people would be free, and he could say ***I'm free, free at last, thank God I'm free at last!*** But all of us here in America, no matter our race, are having our freedom eroded and destroyed by the Federal Government because of its heavy handed tactics. The BLM, the IRS, the NSA—all of the federal agencies are destroying our freedom. I am standing up against their bad and unconstitutional laws, just like Rosa Parks did when she refused to sit in the back of the bus. She started a revolution in America, the civil rights movement, which freed the black people from much of the oppression they were suffering. I'm saying Martin Luther King's dream was not that Rosa could take her rightful seat in the front of the bus, but his dream was that she could take *any* seat on the bus and I would be honored to sit beside her. I am doing the same thing Rosa Parks did—I am standing up against bad laws which dehumanize us and destroy our freedom. Just like the Minutemen at Lexington and Concord. We are saying "No" to an oppressive government which considers us to be slaves rather than free men.

I invite all people in America to join in our peaceful revolution to regain our freedom. That is how America was started, and we need to keep that alive.

--Cliven D. Bundy

The Sharp Family

It was noon and we were just having lunch. Everyone was in the kitchen when I heard a knock at the door. I opened the door and there stood this little woman with long dark hair pulled back from her face into a ponytail on each side. She had a giant smile on her face as she bubbled, "We are the Sharp Family and we have come to sing to you." She said they were from Kansas and one morning two weeks ago she awoke and the Lord told her that she needed to take her family to Nevada to help the Bundy Family. She said she had no idea how they were going to afford to do that because she was a single mother living on $2000 a month with a rent payment of $1,000, She went into the kitchen and told the children about it and they got so excited and said let's go. They said, "Just look up Mom, you always tell us to look up. The Savior will provide." We prayed ourselves here and God is good! It has taken us two weeks because we lost our transmission in Glenwood Springs, Colorado and pulled into a parking lot by a Kentucky Fried Chicken, a Mexican restaurant, and across from a lavish hotel. Some man stopped and gave us $40. She walked over to the hotel to use the phone and find help. The family sang for the manager and he offered to give them a room for the night if they would sing the next day.

She said it was the best night of their whole trip. The hotel gave them a huge suite on the top floor and she took the $40 and bought chicken for the family. They were able to have showers, hot food and a bed to sleep in. The next day a church found them a man who would fix their transmission. They were there for a week getting it repaired. But "Look Up"—we are here to sing for you. I asked where the children were and she pointed to the parking area outside the yard. I told her to go get them and I would get Cliven and Carol. We met just as they were coming through the gate. The ages ranged from 16 down to 4.

We were fully unprepared for what we were about to witness. The family gathered together trying to be in some kind of order and the little boy was moving all about in front and behind and all over the place but as soon as they opened their mouths it was as if the angels in heaven had descended upon us.

Tears began to roll down our cheeks as we felt the Spirit of the Lord begin to engulf us. I have been involved in many beautiful music programs over the years but never have I been touched so deeply by the beautiful harmony and words that were coming from the mouths of these innocent children at that moment! Two hours later and my prayer had been answered! Such faith this woman and her children had. It lifted our spirits and gave us hope again. They had arrived just at the perfect time and on the perfect day. It couldn't have been better planned. The Lord is in charge! We had music for the picnic tonight! It would be a party after all.

Tables were once more set up and the stage was moved under the bridge. Chairs were set up along with the food. The little family sang and each child had been taught to play two musical instruments of their own choosing. There were about 500 people who attended, and those of us who were there were very richly blessed by the music and entertainment provided.

The Sharp Family Singers touched the hearts of everyone at the picnic. We truly felt the angels in heaven had come with them.

The musical Sharp family had stayed at the ranch for about a week, singing, playing and working and having a great time. The mom and children are full of faith and they listen to the Lord. She had said that when the Lord tells her when and what to do then she does it. About 9:00 p.m. as they were getting ready to retire for the night she came into the house and said, "The Lord told me that we need to leave at dusk; when is dusk? They figured out that dusk was between 6:00 p.m. and midnight. Immediately they began to pack their "bus" with their belongings and Cliven and Carol gave them some money so they could travel home safely.

They only made it 45 miles to St. George, Utah when their transmission went out of their van again!

Now what? They called Ryan who was in Cedar City and he came down and picked them up. He took them home to his already crowded little house with his wife and seven children, but they all moved over and made room and welcomed them in. Ryan spent the next week working on rebuilding their transmission. They had an appointment in Kansas to sing for the Governor at the Capital there on our "National Day of Prayer" but they were not going to make it. They decided to come back to the ranch and celebrate "National Prayer Day" at the ranch. We set up the stage by the river and gathered food together again. This time it was very personal and everyone who wanted to be was invited.

The transmission wasn't finished until about 3:00 p.m. so they arrived just after 5:00 p.m. when we were supposed to start. That was alright as we went ahead as soon as we could.

Cliven was invited to attend the Bunkerville Town Hall Meeting that night. They asked him not to allow his body guards to carry their arms inside. As Cliven thought about that, he decided not to attend. How could they allow the Sheriff and his deputies to bring fire arms into a meeting and restrict him? There had been complaint around town about militia men poking around town and stopping people on the road and at check points. Ryan Payne, the head body guard at the Ranch decided to attend the meeting and answer the city councils questions. Sheriff Gillespie and his deputies were there and tried to make Cliven look like a rebel but as soon as Ryan addressed the council he explained the reason why the Militia had to show up. He explained it was because the sheriff refused to do his Constitutional duty to protect his citizens when unarmed Americans are being attacked and deprived of their Constitutional rights—namely 1st Amendment, 2nd Amendment, and so on down the list. He did a wonderful job, and by the time he had finished his speech, the whole City Council was demanding answers from the Sheriff.

We must learn the principles of the Constitution and then abide by its precepts. Have we read the Constitution and pondered it? Are we aware of its principles? Could we defend it? Can we recognize when a law is constitutionally unsound? Abraham Lincoln said, "Let the Constitution be taught in schools, in seminaries, and in colleges, let it be written in primers, in spelling books, in almanacs, let it be preached from the pulpit, proclaimed in legislative halls, and enforced in the courts of justice. Let it become the political religion of the nation."

National Prayer Day Services

The program began with Mrs. Sharp saying a prayer and then the family sang. Then the gathering was opened for others to pray. Ryan Bundy got up and led out with another prayer, then the family sang again. Others got up and prayed and the children each took turns playing their instruments. It was very emotionally moving as one body guard was moved to pray. He said he had never prayed in his life but he did a wonderful job. Another older gentleman dressed in his fatigue laid his hat upon the ground as he knelt upon it and offered up a beautiful prayer. He too had not prayed for a long time. Tears were shed and spirits were full as we ended the beautiful time together.

Afterward we had ice cream and cobbler provided by Cliven's sisters. Delicious! One of the young militia men brought out a guitar and began to play and then another young man played his guitar. The kids joined in and there began to be dancing. Cliven danced with his daughters and everyone had a great time! What a happy day and a great feeling of freedom and peace. Isn't that what life is about?

We must become involved in civic affairs. We cannot do our duty and be idle spectators.

"I, the Lord make you free, therefore ye are free indeed; and the law also maketh you free. Nevertheless, when the wicked rule the people mourn. Wherefore, honest men and wise men shall be sought for

diligently, good men and wise men ye should observe to uphold; otherwise whatsoever is less than these cometh of evil. And I give unto a commandment, that ye shall forsake all evil and cleave unto all good, that ye shall live by every work that proceedeth fourth out of the mouth of God." (D&C 98:8-11)

The qualities that the Lord demands in those who represent us must have all three—good, wise, and honest!

Afterword

That afternoon, while sitting at the kitchen table sorting through the information we had recovered, I received a phone call from Pete Santilli. He told me that he had someone that I really needed to talk to.

He wouldn't tell me who but would call me as soon as they arrived. I had just finished reading through the names of people who were involved with the operation when the call came. I went out the back door so as not to be seen by others. When I came upon Santilli's car he had a young man with him by the name of Jay. Trying to avoid all the militia we made our way out to the trees where the young man's car was parked. Jay opened the trunk and showed us four large white binders full of photos and documents. When he opened the first page he showed me a picture of a man and asked if I had ever seen him before. I answered that the man did look familiar.

He told me that his name was Dr. James Redd. Immediately I remembered some of things about him but I didn't know the whole story. Jay told me that Dr. Redd was his father. Dr. James Redd was the Medical Doctor in Blanding, Utah. They had a big beautiful home on the top of a hill overlooking the town. They had just returned from a family vacation to Rome in October.

The Redd Account

Jay Redd has documented the experience of a federal raid on his parent's home in Blanding to set the record straight on some important details regarding that entire sad experience—

> My mom was a collector and not a trafficker, but again, my dad was neither. Everyone who knows my dad knew he did not collect artifacts. The feds watched him for two and a half years and they also knew he did not collect artifacts but that did not fit the mold the feds had planned for my dad to fit into....
>
> The reason they arrested Dr. Redd on June 10, 2009 was because he picked up off the surface of the ground a tiny little shell bead the feds call an "effigy bird pendant." My dad did not try to sell or trade the tiny little item to the informant or anyone else, he just showed it to him.... The true market value of the bead my dad was arrested for was $75, but the informant and the Feds inflated the price of it over 1250%, saying it was worth $1,000. Now why did they inflate the value? Because the felony charge they gave Dr. Redd required that the item in question, taken from Reservation land, must be valued at over $1,000 in order to qualify as a felony. Anything valued less than $1,000 would be a misdemeanor.
>
> Well, my dad would not have lost his medical license over a misdemeanor, but with a felony he would have and that is what the feds were shooting for.....
>
> The treatment the feds imposed on my dad is beyond disgusting. On June 10, 2009 Dr. Redd was returning home from work (at the hospital) early in the morning. As he drove up to his house he saw numerous black SUVs parked there. As he was pulling up to the driveway one of the agents pointed to his FBI hat, drew his gun and pointed it at him. My dad stopped the vehicle and they yanked him

from his car at gunpoint, handcuffed him (also the agent in charge threatened Dr. Redd that they were going to take away his home, his land, his family and he would never practice medicine, again.) and sat him down in his garage as they milled about him with their weapons...(After over four hours of interrogation sitting on a chair in the middle of his own garage the two agents finally escorted Dr. Redd to the bathroom which he had requested over and over when he first arrived. They took him downstairs and each agent stood six inches from either knee of the doctor, still handcuffed with zip ties, until he was finished and then would not even allowing him to clean himself before they brought him back. They kept asking unreasonable things like, "where's the shovel you like to dig up dead bodies with?" I wonder what the feds said when he requested to speak to his attorney...One of the head agents in charge that day boasted there were 80 agents at my parent's house at one time and throughout the day. (They searched the house for 11 ½ hours) A total of 140 agents visited the house...The agent also said there were seven snipers on my parent's roof for hours and hours waiting for my brother to go down to the house...The day after the raid a resident from Blanding told me he watched my parent's house from a distance with his binoculars and said he saw the agents on the roof not moving for hours and hours... (the agents removed over $500,000 worth of personal property which was never returned.)

Concerning the undercover informant Ted Gardiner: If you read the police report and other articles about his suicide you will see that Ted said he "felt guilty for killing two people." Why would an undercover informant who was supposedly doing his job properly to rid the U.S. of evil underground criminals, feel guilty for the actions of those he caught in a secret, illegal underground activity. Could it be because he made friends with my dad who gave him

> medical advice on his ankle injury, encouraged him a few times to quit smoking to improve his health, invited him to the LDS church function that night....Ted knew he had a major part in Dr. Redd's death and after nine months of torment he could not take it anymore and therefore put a bullet in his head.

Things in quotes below Jay related to me personally:

> After posting this email there was a reply from a Dace Hyatt that same day who says: "Pretty accurate. I was hired to help moderate fair market values on evidence material in Cerberus Action (the government name for this raid), the train wreck briefly described here. The FBI and BLM evidence released in discovery was disturbing to say the least. The lies, corruption and poor form exhibited by many of the agents, prosecution and the CI were in my opinion, crimes that were far more egregious than those committed by the defendants. The ripple effects from all of this is far from over."

The family was traumatized! As his son Jay related the story to us I realized that what he was saying was true. As soon as Dr. Redd had the chance, he made a 45 minute tape and said, "With me gone there will be one less felony" among expressions of love for his family and love of the Lord before he took his own life.

Due to all the torture, threats and lies by these Agents toward Dr. Redd, they caused his death.

At his funeral a General Authority quoted John 15:13—"Greater love hath no man than this, that a man lay down his life for his friends"—and D&C 101:35-38—"And all they who suffer persecution for my name, and endure in faith, though they are called to lay down their lives for my sake yet shall they partake of all this glory. Wherefore, fear not even unto death; for in this world your joy is not full, but in me your joy is full. Therefore, care not for the body, neither the life of the body; but care for the soul, and the life of the soul. And seek the face of the Lord always, that in patience ye shall have eternal life.

The undercover informant, Ted Gardiner, told a friend a few days before he killed himself that he wanted to distance himself from the whole undercover operation. He gave the friend a coin that was given to all the agents involved which reads "Cerberus Action" with "BLM—2009—FBI" and the picture of a three headed dog/wolf printed on it. A year or so later, Ted's friend gave the coin to Jay, Dr. Redd's son.

<u>More Horror Stories</u>

In my own town, I had someone about that time who had gone out on the Paiute Reservation and was digging up an Indian pot he found and even though he was alone he was met by the Federal Agents by the time he arrived home that evening and arrested. They have the capability of "Google Earth" where they can literally zoom in on someone anywhere, anytime.

We had a man who got a $10,000 fine for running over some sagebrush off the edge of the road out on the Escalante National Monument.

There was a local businessmen and his wife who were about to retire from their Sand and Rock excavation business when one day they decided to go for a ride on their four wheeler up on the Kaibab Mountain. They were driving along an old abandoned logging road that he and his father built for the logging company years ago. It was kind of grown over and it ran alongside a fence. At the bottom of a little hill was a woman in a government vehicle. She stopped them and asked them what they were doing. They explained to her that they were just out for a little ride. She proceeded to tell them that it was illegal to drive on that road and that they had run over some brush. She wrote them out a citation and they had to appear in Court in Flagstaff. The Court really threw the book at them and after months of court hearings and attorney fees the judge reduced their gigantic fine to $70,000. It almost killed them off both physically and emotionally. The stress has caused them terrible health issues to this day.

Another group of young men who are dedicated hikers had gone on an overnight camping trip to the Turoweep Canyon in the Arizona Desert. They had moved a log and driven a few feet off the dirt road and during the night it got extremely cold, they built a small fire and burned one little sagebrush. Immediately at daybreak a ranger appeared and threatened to arrest them all and write them heavy citations. They negotiated with the ranger and pleaded for mercy. They offered their services to help do work for restoration. Because they were young and strong the ranger took them up on it and required them to work for a full week hiking up and down the canyon from sun up to sun down hauling trash and building walk ways. It was very hard work and they said that even though they were in good shape they thought, it really beat them up physically.

Who are these people who have usurped this kind of power? They can close down our roads, restrict access to our public lands, and police our people? That is taxation without representation! We can't even vote them out.

Dr. Redd's son, Jay, has filed a law suit against the Special Agent in Charge, Daniel P. Love. When Jay heard the name "Daniel P. Love" Special Agent in Charge was the man leading the attack at the Bundy Ranch on the Santilli Show, he immediately contacted Pete and this was the story he shared with us.

Jay has spent years gathering information about this man and his friend "Barnes." The moment those names left his mouth I immediately went inside and retrieved a copy of the list of people who were involved because I remembered both of those names were on it. There were other names he also recognized.

Daniel P. Love was the same man who three different people had told me that whenever they were in his presence and spoke with him they all had feelings of darkness and evil. Some said he was a very wicked man and others said he was the devil. I had taken photos of him without knowing it, but I had never met him before. At the Bundy Standoff he was recorded saying, "The Government owns the cattle and if I want to shoot all the cattle and bury them in a hole I can do it!"

A Testimony of Pete Santilli from GuerillaMediaNetwork .com—

On April 11th, I went to Daniel P. Love for what I knew was my last contact with him. Although I found him to be such an idiot for making the statements he made to me in the days prior, I sincerely wanted to appeal to his compassion, and possibly break through and disarm what I believed to be a human ticking time bomb. I was very focused on conveying the following message: "The people who have come here are families; women; children, determined; and will not negotiate for anything which gives up their God given freedoms." I told him that he should consider and direct to his staff that they have an opportunity – and that the moment I was describing would certainly come; that the people would come unarmed and determined to free the cattle, and ask them to leave —he should take the opportunity to consider that the people he would be confronted by are peaceful and Constitutional, and he and his people should stand down in favor of the U.S. Constitution and humans exercising their Constitutional rights. His response is chillingly clear in the audio. He said, "That ain't gonna happen, and you better have more people than you do now, because we have enough guys to have you all rounded up and arrested."

(http://guerillamedianetwork.com/released-more-secret-audio-of-blm-special-agent-in-charge-daniel-p-love-transcript/)

Lawsuit

In the lawsuit of "ESTATE OF JAMES D. REDD.M.D., et. al., Plaintiff, DANIEL LOVE, et. al., Defendants, Dace D. Hyatt gives very damning evidence that shows his credibility with 22 years of experience in the antiquities market and the field of Native American artifacts. He bought and then sold collections to Ted Gardiner. Prior to Cerberus Action he sold Ted Gardiner countless artifacts, some of which were comparable to the drilled bird head known now as the bird effigy pendant. Never in his dealings with Ted did he sell a comparable or even slightly more valuable item in excess of $150. He is prepared to locate multiple transaction receipts in his records between 2000 and 2008.

"I have seen and evaluated the bird-effigy pendent that was the subject of the government's investigation, known as Cerberus Action, in context to Dr. James Redd. Based on my evaluation, the value of the bird-effigy pendant is $75." This was signed and dated November 14, 2012 by Dace D. Hyatt and filed with this law suit.

As I began to research Dan Love, I discovered many incidents that he has been involved in with many people that I know. There are many people who have issue with his tactics and ethics, including sheriffs, commissioners, and state representatives. He works under the employment of the Special Agent Division Head, Salvatore Lauro, who is under Ken Salazar, head of the Department of Interior over minerals and mining and who is one of President Obama's appointees. They admire and praise Daniel P. Love—imagine that!

Many people want to call some of the American people "Conspiracy Theorists" like it is a terrible thing. The reality is "history repeats itself!" There are conspiring men among us. To quote scripture:

But behold, Satan did stir up the hearts of the more part of the [people], *insomuch that they did unite with those bands of robbers, and did enter into their covenants and their oaths that they would protect and preserve one another in whatsoever difficult circumstances they should be placed, that they should not suffer for their murders, and their plunderings, and their stealings.*

And it came to pass that they did have their secret signs yea, their secret signs, and their secret words; and this that they might distinguish a brother who had entered into the covenant, that whatsoever wickedness his brother should do he should not be injured by his brother, nor by those who did belong to his band, who had taken this covenant.

And thus they might murder, and plunder, and steal, and commit whoredoms and all manner of wickedness, contrary to the laws of their country and also the laws of their God.

And whosoever of those who belonged to their band should reveal unto the world of their wickedness and their abominations, should be tried, not according to the laws of their country, but according to the laws of their wickedness, which had been given by Gadianton and Kishkumen.

Now behold, it is these secret oaths and covenants which Alma commanded his son should not go forth unto the world, let they should be a means of bringing down the people unto destruction.

Now behold, these secret oaths and covenants did not come forth unto Gadianton from the records which were delivered unto Helaman; but behold, they were put into the heart of Gadianton by that same being who did entice our first parents to partake of the forbidden fruit—

Yea, that same being who did plot with Cain, that if he would murder his brother Abel it should not be known unto the world. And he did plot with Cain and his followers from that time forth.

And also it is that same being who put it in the hearts of the people to build a tower sufficiently high that they might get to heaven. And it was that same being who led on the people who came from that tower into this land; who spread the works of darkness and abominations over all the face of the land, until he dragged the people down to an entire destruction, and to an everlasting hell.

Yea, it is that same being who put it into the heart of Gadianton to still carry on the work of darkness, and of secret murder; and he has brought it forth from the beginning of man even down to this time.

And behold, it is he who is the author of all sin. And behold he doth carry on his works of darkness and secret murder, and doth hand down their plots, and their oaths, and their covenants, and their plans of awful wickedness, from generation to generation according as he can get hold upon the hearts of the children of men.

And now behold, he had got great hold upon the hearts of the Nephites; yea insomuch that they had become exceedingly wicked; yea, the more part of them. (Helaman 6: 21-31 from the Book of Mormon)

Everything stated above occurred in 29 BC here on the American Continent.

Did President Obama not take the oath of office when he became President? "I do solemnly swear (or affirm) that I will faithfully execute the Office of President of the United States, and will to the best of my Ability, preserve, protect and defend the Constitution of the United States."

Has he done that?

How many men have taken that Oath and yet they trample upon the Constitution and disregard it altogether? The Lord will hold them accountable and so should we!

We must make our influence felt by our vote, our letters, and our advice.

- We must be wisely informed and let others know how we feel.
- We must take part in local precinct meetings and select delegates who truly represent our feelings.

In 1831, the Lord said in these latter-days—

> *For behold, it is not meet that I should command in all things; for he that is compelled in all things, the same is a slothful and not a wise servant; wherefore he receiveth no reward. Verily I say, men should be anxiously engaged in a good cause, and do many things of their own free will, and bring to pass much righteousness; For the power is in them, wherein they are agents unto themselves. And inasmuch as men do good they shall in nowise lose their reward. But he that does not anything until he is commanded, and receiveth a commandment with doubtful heart, and keepeth it with slothfulness, the same is damned.* (D&C 58:26-29)

Intent to File Charges

Signs and evidence—

This is a map of the operation set up on the Bundy Ranch.

It was on May 2, 2014 that we decided we needed to go to the sheriff's office in Las Vegas and file charges against the Agents who had attacked family members and friends at gun point and put innocent people's lives in danger.

The media were all there and Ammon made a wonderful speech to them—

Dear Sheriff Gillespie,

Your latest comments and references in local news outlets have compelled this response. You have continuously pointed fingers at Cliven Bundy and the BLM saying they are both to blame for the incident at the Bundy Ranch. You said the BLM lied to you and Cliven Bundy brought armed men to the ranch to protect himself. These accusations (as you know) are just further lies and manipulations. However, the main concern in all these embracing, untruthful and self-serving comments is you never point the finger at yourself. You do not even take one small portion of responsibility. It may be understood that you are a politician first, a law enforcer second, and somewhere way down the line a public servant who is here to protect the people, but your action and lack of responsibility for them takes the cake.

We ask you this one question: *What are the people to do?*

What are they to do when hundreds of unauthorized fully armed agents come into their community and terrorize them, occupying an entire multilevel hotel, putting perimeters around it and patrolling it, right in the middle of their town, threatening anyone by force if they even so much as come close to the grounds? What are the people to do when these hired federal mercenaries lock up the land by gun point and say it is theirs? Land that had been carved out for generations with the sweat and blood of the very people that are being locked out and threatened with force if they do so much as step off the paved road. What are the people to do when snipers hired by the Bureau of Land Management (BLM) put their cross hairs on them while others point guns in the faces of their loved ones, even women holding infants? What are the people to do when their beloved community member is gang beaten to the ground, kicked, stomped on, fist punched, guard dogs ordered to attack and then paraded around for hours like a trophy simply for filming these people with his iPad? What are the people to do when they are met with excessive force if they even so much as raise a sign to protest against the actions of these armed, overzealous militants hired by their own government? What are the people to do when these dedicated heavy forces covertly begin by backhoe to destroy the water heads and infrastructure on the mountains that were put in by the people and their forefathers over a hundred years ago?

We ask you sheriff, *what are the people to do?*

What are they to do when protesting against these horrific acts they are thrown to the ground, tasered and have vicious trained dogs ordered to attack them? What are they to do when they call 911 for emergency medical assistants and you, Sheriff Gillespie, have told the emergency services and your deputies not to assist in anyway? What are they to do when their teenage boys are tackled to the ground and beaten for crossing some imaginary line? If you look into the action of these heavy-handed impersonators you will find that we have not exaggerated any of their actions, in-fact we have not explained even the half of it. So again what are a people to do in these circumstances? Are they to hang their heads and let these atrocities continue simply because it is their Federal Government that is the offender?

Let me tell you what they should do. They should call on their County Sheriff to protect them, and he should come by any means available to shield the people and protect their rights. Sheriff Gillespie, we did called on you! Almost a hundred recorded times. We begged, pleaded, and even demanded that you come and end the action of these law breaking, over-reaching federally hired militants. Each time you refused, you chose to play politics and sided with the aggressive offenders because of their power and what it might mean to you later on.

You could have ended it at any time, even before it began. You premeditated to reject the people and stand with those who would take our rights away with pointed guns, padding your political pocket. And now you are desperately trying to save face by pinning the injustice on those that are in the right. You and people like you, *are* the problem. You are an example of why the people are trusting government less and less. We the people hired you to protect our lives, our liberties and our property. The incident at the Bundy Ranch has proven that you are not willing to do any of these things. In fact, you did just opposite. You put our lives, our liberties and our properties in jeopardy. Your actions (and the lack of) forced we the people to do your job and stand against the threat of federally pointed guns. You left it to the people to rid themselves of these historically oppressive actions. It is the people's duty to protect their rights, but to keep order we have authorized and hired you to do it for us. In this you have failed.

It is truly sad that one as powerful and seasoned as yourself does not even begin to understand the purpose of government, including your own position. For most of your adult life you have sworn to uphold and defend the U.S. Constitution. You have also been elected to protect the lives, liberties and property of the people who live and come into the county. When the people needed your protection (due to gross violation of the Constitution) you chose to seek more power and assist the very violators that would give it to you, forgetting the people and your sworn duty to them.

We warn you and other politicians that lead or follow your example, the people are in unrest because of your type of actions. The purpose of government is to protect the unalienable rights of the people, not to take them away. It is the duty of the people to defend their God-given rights if governments fail to do so or turns to discard them. Good and civil citizens wish only to live in tranquility and peace, but demand freedom while doing so. We call upon you and all civil servants to effectuate the true purpose of government and change your actions as needed by fulfilling your sworn oath and duty to the Constitution and ultimately to the people.

—Ammon Bundy

Charges Filed

Then we all filed in and filled out our reports. We were swarmed with media and as I sat amongst the sisters helping to fill out our reports a reporter kept trying to ask questions. He finally said his name was Ken Ritter with Associated Press. At that instant I figured it out, I had been setting up interviews with him for CNN until I discovered that they were the ones who put the spin on Cliven about the so called "Racist" issue.

I looked at the sisters and said, "We don't talk to them, they are the ones who spun the remarks calling Cliven a racist!" He tried to explain that he just reported and didn't spin it. I told him it was from his Media and we weren't doing any more interviews with them. He tried again but the girls all turned their backs on him and said, "We're not talking to you!" He finally left.

We believe that men should appeal to the civil law for redress of all wrongs and grievances, where personal abuse is inflicted or the right of property or character infringed, where such laws exist as will protect the same; but we believe that all men are justified in defending themselves, their friends, and property, and the government, from the unlawful assaults and encroachments of all persons in times of exigency, where immediate appeal cannot be made to the laws, and relief afforded.

(D&C 134:11)

When asked, "Then do you profess to ignore the laws of the land?" John Taylor (President of the LDS Church from October 1880 to July 1887) answered, "No; not unless they are unconstitutional, then I would do it all the time. Whenever the Congress of the United States, for instance, passes a law interfering with my religion, or with my religious rights. I will read a small portion of that instrument called the Constitution of the United States, now almost obsolete, which says 'Congress shall pass no law interfering with religion or the free exercise thereof' [US Constitutional Amendment 1]; and I would say, gentleman, you may go to Gibraltar with your law, and I will live my religion. When you become violators of the Constitution you have sworn before high heaven to uphold, and perjure yourselves before God, then I will maintain the right, and leave you to take the wrong just as you please."

Joseph Smith said: "The Constitution is not a law, but it empowers the people to make laws... The Constitution tells us what shall not be a lawful tender... The legislature has ceded up to us the privilege of enacting such laws as are not inconsistent with the Constitution of the United States... The different states, and even Congress itself, have passed many laws diametrically contrary to the Constitution of the United States..."

We went to our lawyer's office and asked to have a prayer before we began.

Lawyers

On this same American Continent there was a time when the people became so wicked they began to destroy the righteous because they refused to obey God and keep his commandments. They also couldn't bear to have their sins pointed out, so there began to arise many lawyers who twisted the words to condemn the righteous. These are the warnings of the prophet Amulek of that day that were given to the people then which fits our day today—

"Oh ye wicked and perverse generation, ye lawyers and ye hypocrites, for ye are laying the foundations of the devil; for ye are laying traps and snares to catch the holy ones of God. Ye are laying plans to pervert the ways of the righteous, and to bring down the wrath of God upon your heads, even to the utter destruction of this people."

The King at that time, Mosiah, said, *"... if the time should come that the voice of this people should choose iniquity, that is, if the time should come that this people should fall into transgression, they would be ripe for destruction."* The prophet Amulek continued,

"And now I say unto you that well doth the Lord judge of your iniquities; well doth he cry unto this people, by the voice of his angels: Repent ye, repent, for the kingdom of heaven is at hand. Yea, well doth he cry, by the voice of his angels that: I will come down among my people, with equity and justice in my hands. Yea, and I say unto you that if it were not for the prayers of the righteous, who are now in the land, that ye would even now be visited with utter destruction; yet it would not be by flood, as were the people in the days of Noah, but it would be by famine, and by pestilence, and the sword.

"But it is by the prayers of the righteous that ye are spared; now therefore, if ye will cast out the righteous from among you then will not the Lord stay his hand; but in his fierce anger he will come out against you; then ye shall be smitten by famine, and by pestilence, and by the sword: and the time is soon at hand except ye repent." (Alma 10: 17-23)

The people hated Amulek for saying these things, so Amulek stretched forth his hand and said,

"O ye wicked and perverse generation, why hath Satan got such great hold upon your hearts? Why will ye yield yourselves unto him that he may have power over you, to blind your eyes, that ye will not understand the words which are spoken, according to their truth? For behold, have I testified against your law? Ye do not understand; ye say that I have spoken against your law; but I have not, but I have spoken in favor of your law [Constitution] *to your condemnation. And now behold, I say unto you, that the foundation of the destruction of this people is beginning to be laid by the unrighteousness of your lawyers and your judges."* (Alma 10:25-27)

Now the object of these lawyers was to get gain; and they got gain according to their employ. (Alma 10:32)

Check it out, because I believe that describes our day today.

Domestic Terrorists

This Bundy Ranch Cattle Battle is not over! Senator Harry Reid said it's not over when he called us all domestic terrorists. Graig Leff, a spokesperson for the BLM has stated, "We'll figure out how to go forward on this." He added that, "The BLM did not participate in the negotiations that de-escalated the tension. The BLM and National Park Service did not cut any deal or negotiate anything." Our very own Senator Harry Reid has stated the Federal Government cannot let citizens disobey the law and not pay for it. This tyrannical Federal Government not only makes unconstitutional laws for the citizens, they have exempted themselves from having to obey any Constitutional law and pick and choose what laws they want to uphold. We are losing our freedoms daily!

> *"Will the Constitution be destroyed? No. It will be held inviolate by the people; and as Joseph Smith said, 'The time will come when the Destiny of this nation will hang upon a single thread, and at this critical juncture, this people will step forth and save it from the threatened destruction.'*
>
> *"It will be so. I do not know when that day will come or how it will come to pass. I feel sure that when it does come to pass, among those who will step forward from among this people will be men who hold the Holy Priesthood and who carry as credentials a bachelor or doctor of law degree. And women also, of honor. And there will be Judges as well.*
>
> *Others from the world outside the Church will come, as Colonel Thomas Kane did, and bring with them their knowledge of the law to protect this people.*
>
> *We may one day stand alone, but we will not change or lower our standards, or change our course."* (Boyd K. Packer 2004 "On the Shoulders of Giants," Brigham Young University, J. Rueben Clark Law Society Devotional, Saturday, 2-28-04, 6:00 p.m.)

Each of you knows what the Lord has inspired you to do. You each need to pray and take action now. We need to stand up together!

<u>One Man's Opinion</u>

Bryan Hyde is a news commentator and co-host of the Perspectives talk show on Fox News 1450 AM 93.1 FM. He is also a personal friend of mine. On March 31, 2014 Bryan wrote an opinion piece that is shared below—

The name Bundy is a familiar one in this part of the American West. Right now it's a name that many are hearing thanks to a longstanding cattle dispute with the federal Bureau of Land Management.

I have personally known Ryan Bundy for many years. I consider him a friend and a good man. I feel the same way about his father Cliven. These are men who are well acquainted with hard work and who are willing to stand for liberty when others are unwilling.

The Bundy's are down-to-earth people. They don't use big words to impress or try to couch their ideas in pseudo-intellectual language. They speak with simplicity. This makes them unsympathetic figures to some.

But it would be very foolish to mistake them for uniformed troublemakers who don't understand government's proper limits. They are the last of dozens of area ranchers who have resisted being regulated out of existence by the BLM. One by one, other cattlemen have been forced to abandon their livelihood by an increasingly unreasonable bureaucracy.

Stripped of all the emotional posturing and misdirection, the core principle at stake here is a simple one. Either our Federal Government exists to protect and guarantee our rights of life, liberty, or the pursuit of happiness or it does not.

It's not just the Bundy's property and liberty that are at stake. There are larger implications for all of us. But relatively few Americans recognize why this is so.

Cliven Bundy and his family know what many Americans don't yet know. They know what it's like to fight for your livelihood against a corrupted bureaucracy. Understanding the Bundy's stance requires some historical perspective.

Water and forage rights, and a host of other land use rights are all based in the legal concept of beneficial use. This refers to the right held by a person who has equitable title to real property to utilize that real property while another holds the legal title.

This is what the Bundy family has done for 130 years. While engaging in beneficial use, they have developed the land and made improvements that have benefited wildlife. Most importantly, they have caused no harm.

So why is a federal bureaucracy so intent on bringing them to heel? Because the nature of unaccountable power is to become progressively oppressive and dictatorial.

Is the BLM protecting rights and property when it issues complicated legal rules and proclamations to restrict public access to these lands? Is the BLM serving the American people by making rules when no one is looking?

Do bureaucratic tools like controlled public hearings filled with statistical pseudo-expertise serve the interests of the public or that of the system? Why are we progressively seeing our public lands place out of reach with a permit?

Shall "We the People" govern ourselves or be at the mercy of elitists and bureaucrats in some far off district to make those decisions for us? Who is the servant and who is the master?

Michael Rozeff sums up why this is a stand worth making: "A bureaucracy can outlast a person and wear him down. Only a very unusual and heroic member of the public is willing to spend his or her life fighting these bureaucracies and rousing the public."

Cliven Bundy's courageous stance, coupled with his family's spirit of rugged individualism tendencies has enraged the federal supremacists among us. Critics fume in contrived outrage that the

Bundys are violating BLM regulations by grazing their cattle on federal land without a permit. Never mind that the Bundys have lawfully possessed the water and forage rights for generations. Because they have refused to apply and pay for a newly required government permit, the feds now intend to steal their cattle. Like all tyrants, they do it under the color of law.

Those who openly or tacitly support these authoritarian actions are a perfect example of our society-wide ethical breakdown.

We have been conditioned to view government policies only in terms of "legal" or "illegal" but never in terms of rights. Rights are what limit government's power over us. Those who stand accused of illegality by someone in power are pressed to have no rights.

Eric Peters writes: "It doesn't matter—that is, it is no 'legal' defense—to point out that the 'illegal' act has not caused any harm to anyone. Anything—literally, anything—the state decrees to be 'illegal' is by definition, sufficient 'legal' pretext to vitiate our rights."

Those who think this is about a family of scofflaws getting their comeuppance are missing the point.

Is our government still accountable to the people who created it? Or have we become the subjects?

If the Bundys can be legally deprived of life, liberty, and property for having caused no harm, it can be done to anybody.
(Bryan Hyde)

On bended knee we must:

- Pray to help us restore our Constitution the way it was set up by our Founding Fathers.
- Pray for the leaders of this nation lead us righteously.

- Pray to help us become a righteous and moral people once more.
- Pray to bless this nation to return to God.

Then Stand Up and Do All You Can!

Our lives, our Children, and all of our Posterity's lives depend on it!

Follow Up

Since this battle, Cliven has joined the Independent American Party (IAP) and has spoken to hundreds of groups across the Western States. Last weekend he said, *"This is an age-old battle between good and evil. There are people from almost every State in this United States here. Some have told me they'd traveled for 40 hours to get here. So why did they come? It was because they felt like they needed to. They had been spiritually touched."*

He also asked if our Constitution was an inspired document by Jesus Christ. Of course, we all said, "Yes." *"Isn't it scripture then?"* he asked. *"The same as the Bible or Book of Mormon?"* He explained that even though we were unarmed people facing those guns, we prayed for help. If we were wrong then why was the Lord with us? Why did he send the flocks of geese? Could the people have stood without fear without the Lord's help? When they returned back to the Check Point area, I noticed the light that was in them and the joy and happiness they brought from that experience. ***The Lord told me, "If the sheriff doesn't disarm those federal agents, We the People will have to face these arms again in a civil war."***

Again, the message he gave me to give everyone was—

Tell your sheriff to disarm every federal bureaucrat in your county. They have no policing authority. If he refuses to do that, then he is not a Constitutional sheriff and this is the year to replace him with someone who is.

Now you have all been warned!

CLOSING REMARKS

ॐ

From Briana Bundy, wife of Cliven's son Mel

I was driving home from the ranch and I was thinking about the things that had transpired on the hill the day before. I remembered that Cliven had asked us all to make an account of the things we had witnessed for our posterity. I could only think of the moment on the hill when Clancy took command and told us what would happen. I felt the ground shake beneath me, it was so powerful. I tried to recall his words but knew it could never do him justice. I needed every word. I grabbed a pen and paper and began to ponder and my hand was taken over and I began to write. A description of Clancy poured onto the page at the moment I wrote, "And these were his words." Clancy's voice filled my car with the same power he exuded on the hill. This is my account—

As a man of honor, courage and conviction,
Clancy Cox stopped.
He gathered the riders around.
His horse stood at the head.
He was commanding and confident.
His horse moved from left to right.
His reins held tight.
His posture was mighty.
The flag of Moroni flapped in the wind above his hat.
His face was solid.
His eyes did not lose contact with his riders.

These were his words:
"This is what we're gonna do!
We're gonna stay in a line!
You are not to speak to anyone!
You are not going to be confrontational!
You will provoke no one!
We are here with God on our side!
Some of you may be atheist, I don't know.
I don't want to offend anyone.
But I believe in God, and He WILL protect us!
Once we get to the wash, we're gonna fan out!
We will form a wall and advance to the gate!
We will remain reverent!
We will stand our ground and we will not waiver!
We will show no fear!
We will be victorious and that will be by God!
We will uphold the Constitution of our Forefathers!
And THEY will be with us!
LET'S GO!!"

—Clancy Cox, April 12, 2014

Clancy with the Title of Liberty

I am so grateful to have the opportunity to receive these words for our children and grandchildren. Clancy Cox is a man of greatness and should be honored accordingly. His spirit is an asset to our family and I am proud that I had the chance to ride by his side.

This experience has taught me that there is no limitation to the amount of faith we can receive. Thank you, Cliven, for being a man of faith, principle and integrity, and leading this family the way that I know was pleasing to the Lord.

I love you all more than you know and I believe our family bond became so strong Saturday that no one or no thing can ever break it.

Proudly and humbly,

Briana Bundy

From Shawna Cox

In June I was repairing a roof and fell, shattering my heel bone. I have been laid up literally with my foot over my heart for 90 days with screws and metal plates. I believe that the Lord needed me to get this book written as a testimony and it would not have happened if He didn't slow me down.

Thanks to my husband, Don for waiting on me and having so much patience.

Thanks also to David Tuttle and his wife for putting me up and putting up with me through all this.

Thanks to my wonderful friend Lynette and my ward members and friends and neighbors for taking such good care of me.

This book was written as a Testimony of my own. I pray that people will forgive my mistakes as I am only human and subject to err. This I do know for certain. God was there. He was at the Ranch House; He was at the Wash. He was with the Cowboys and the people over and under the bridge. He stands supreme for this is His Country. Just like He brought together the wisest men on the Earth to create the Constitution of this Land and many have died to save it. We are only a free people when we obey Him and stay Moral and Righteous. We must turn from our evil ways and follow after Him. I know God lives and loves us. I pray for all of us, that we may listen to His promptings and obey them. We will be held accountable if we do not.

Shawna Cox

To follow the ongoing saga with the Bundy family in Bunkerville, NV visit and subscribe to the Bundy Blog:

http://bundyranch.blogspot.com/

To follow the more recent events that unfolded in Burns, Oregon culminating in the unwarranted death of fellow patriot, LaVoy Finicum visit:

http://www.onecowboysstandforfreedom.com